Learning With Raffi

Singable Songs

(The Famous Raffi Songs,
(Learning Activities, Patterns, Props,
and Creative-Play Ideas)

by
Sherrill B. Flora

Illustrated by
Gary Hoover

Publisher
Instructional Fair • TS Denison
Grand Rapids, Michigan 49544

Credits:
Author: Sherrill B. Flora
Editorial Consultant: Bert Simpson
Illustration Artist: Gary Hoover
Book Cover Design: Annette Hollister-Papp
The art was taken from the original recording jacket, designed by Raffi
Music Typesetting: Chris Murray
Music Editor: Faith Carriere
Child Illustrations: Kassie Flora

Standard Book Number:1-56822-570-9
UPC: 0-13587-20504-1
SPCN: 590-219-1432
Learning with Raffi – Singable Songs

2400 Turner Avenue NW
Grand Rapids, Michigan 49544
Printed in the USA

Contents

❖ ❖ ❖ A Special Message From Raffi ❖ ❖ ❖

Young children learn from everything they do, and as a children's entertainer I've come to understand how naturally and easily they learn from singing. They love to hear and sing their favorite songs over and over, and the repetition and predictable patterns of my songs make them "singable" and easy to remember. As children listen, sing, and move to the music, they are internalizing the concepts - story, sequence, number, rhythm and movement, rhyme - that underlie every area of learning.

The words to my songs touch upon topics that are part of children's everyday lives, and can therefore provide natural springboards to further exploration and learning. The activities in this book have been designed to build on the familiar and extend easily and naturally into new, less familiar areas. As we know, this is how young children, like the rest of us, learn best.

Whether you use this book at home or at school, I hope you will enjoy my songs and the fun you can have with them. Happy singing and learning!

Raffi

❖ ❖ ❖ Introduction ❖ ❖ ❖

Parents and teachers have always known how easily and joyfully young children respond to music. Music in the early childhood classroom is an integral part of curriculum. Music is often used throughout the day to introduce, teach, and reinforce many basic concepts and readiness skills. Parents have used music as a means to entertain, delight, and enrich learning experiences. As children sing their favorite songs over and over and over again, they are actually internalizing new concepts and increasing basic skills, self-confidence, and self-esteem, as well as building a foundation for further growth of academic readiness.

Raffi epitomizes excellence in children's music. His songs enchant children, while the repetition of verses and patterns, and rhythm and rhyme, enable children to learn the words rapidly. *Learning with Raffi – Singable Songs* will provide you with the sheet music, lyrics, and activities that reinforce and enhance the concepts of each song. The book is filled with patterns that can be used for creative and dramatic play activities. *Learning with Raffi – Singable Songs* takes the best of children's music and gives the teacher or parent ideas on how to teach with Raffi's music, and how to effectively use music throughout a child's learning environment.

Song 1

The More We Get Together

Use this song with these themes:

Friendship

Cooperation

Welcome

Self-Esteem

Cultural Diversity

Tolerance

Materials to be used with these activities:

Polaroid Camera

Paper Plates

Crayons

Markers

Scissors

Construction Paper

Scrap Box

Tongue Depressors

About This Song

Traditional

Copyright © 1976 Homeland Publishing (CAPAC)

Whether you teach at an early childhood program, a child care center, or at home, *The More We Get Together* is a wonderful song to use during "circle time" or during your "first activities" of the day. The words and warm attitudes used in this song can help ease children into their day. "The more we get together, the happier we'll be," and "your friends are my friends" are powerful messages that tell children that they are in a safe and nurturing environment.

Use this song in the morning and watch smiles light up your learning environment.

The More We Get Together

Polaroid Picture Fun

Let the children enjoy taking pictures of one another. Even four and five year olds can understand how to take a picture. A polaroid camera provides for "instant" fun and success. Once you have allowed the children to take pictures, there are a variety of activities that can be used with the photographs:

1. Pass out the pictures to the children, making sure that no one has their own picture. The children walk around the room and find the person in the picture that they are holding.
2. The child looks at a photograph and then describes the person. The other children have to guess who the child is describing.
3. Make a photo display. Mount the photographs in construction paper frames and display on a bulletin board or wall. Caption your display "YOUR FRIENDS ARE MY FRIENDS." Let the children sing the song "The More We Get Together" and then name all their friends.

I Am A Special Friend Because . . . (Paper Plate People)

Provide each of the children with a paper plate. (The *Chinet* brand works the best because it is so sturdy.) Cut out eye holes in the plate for the children. Let the children add facial features, color the skin, glue yarn for hair, and add anything extra they may find in your scrap box (earrings, scarfs, sequins, buttons, etc.).

Attach the paper plates to tongue depressors or paint stir sticks (often available free-of-charge at your local hardware store). The children can hold the puppet in front of their own face.

On the tongue depressor or stick that you are using for the puppet handle, ask the children to dictate to you, or print for themselves, a short sentence describing why she or he feels that they know how to be a special friend to someone.

Friends

(written by Louise Binder Scott)

A poem to memorize and dramatize

I have two friends,	(hold up two fingers on left hand)
And they have me	(hold up one finger on right hand)
Two friends and me,	(bend each from left to right)
That's one, two, three.	(hold up while saying "1, 2, 3")

Ask the children to describe their best friend. What makes this friend so special? What types of activities do they enjoy playing with their best friend? Will this person always be their best friend?

Friendship Boxes

This is an inexpensive and easy-to-make gift idea. Find a small box. Cover the box in wrapping paper, or create your own wrapping paper from discarded grocery bags. Tie a beautiful bow on the package.

Make a gift card that says; "Do not unwrap this gift! The box is filled with love. Just hold the box and you will feel our friendship!" (This is a fun gift to make for grandparents, parents, and other special people.)

Friends To The End

A Venn diagram can be a great tool to use for comparing and contrasting. In this activity, use the Venn diagram to discover what you and your special friend have in common. You will also discover that you may have some differences. Use the following example to make your Venn diagram.

Friends Forever Fruit Salad

Have students work in pairs to create this wonderful "Friends Forever Fruit Salad."

You will need: 1 banana, 10 grapes, 1 apple, 1 orange (peeled), and a dull knife (to be used with adult supervision).

Here is what you do: Slice the banana, apple, and orange into small bite-size pieces. Cut each grape in half. The friends should decide who is going to do what job. For example, the first child can cut the apple and orange while the second child cuts the banana and the grapes.

Enjoy a picnic together!

Friends!

The children can use this pattern to create a picture of themselves or their friends. On the front of the t-shirt the children can print (or dictate to you) a sentence about friendship.

Song 2

Down By The Bay

Use this song with these themes:

Rhyming

Memory Skills

Animals

Make-Believe

❖❖❖❖❖❖❖❖❖❖

Materials to be used with these activities:

Paper

Scissors

Crayons

Markers

Posterboard

Stapler

Down By The Bay (Picture Book)

About This Song

Traditional

If you are the parent of a young child or are teaching in an early childhood program, you undoubtedly know the song *Down By The Bay*. It is a traditional song, sung in most pre-school and kindergarten programs.

Down By The Bay introduces children to the concept of rhyming through the use of silly ideas and wonderful visual appeal. "Did you ever see a goose kissing a moose?" is an easy image to visualize and fun enough that a child would really like to see it. Make up your own verse to *Down By The Bay*. Use the names of the children in your learning environment or use the names of their family members.

Down By The Bay

2. Did you ever see a whale with a polka-dot tail...
3. Did you ever see a fly wearing a tie...
4. Did you ever see a bear combing his hair...
5. Did you ever see llamas eating their pajamas...
6. Did you ever have a time when you couldn't make a rhyme...

Down by the bay.

Down By The Bay Visual Cards

Enlarge and copy, color, and laminate all of *Down By The Bay* Cards, found on pages 10 -12. Let the children take turns holding up the cards as you sing each verse of the song. The children may also wish to make their own *Down By The Bay* Books. This is a wonderful tool for emergent readers. As the children sing and follow along with the words in the book, they will soon be able to identify and read many of the words. The children can add their own verses and illustrate their own pictures.

An Echo Song

Down By The Bay is a terrific song to teach and sing with echoes. The instructor can sing a line (down by the bay) and the children echo the exact line. The entire song of *Down By The Bay* can be sung with echoes.

Divide the group of children into two teams. Team one will sing first and will sing loudly - team 2 will echo each line softly. Switch so each team gets an opportunity to sing both loud and soft.

Down By The Bay - A Song To Read

Children will love to read and sing along with the picture book, *Down By The Bay,* (1987, Crown Publishers, Inc., NY), part of the Raffi Songs To Read™ series. The illustrations show two friends playing a game in which they imagine the silly scenes from the song happening in their own home. Turn the pages and sing together. Have the book available when the children to follow along as they listen to Raffi's recording.

Down by the bay,

1

where the watermelons grow,

2

back to my home,
I dare not go

3

for if I do,
my mother will say:

4

Did you ever see a goose
kissing a moose . . .

5

Did you ever see a whale
with a polka-dot tail . . .

6

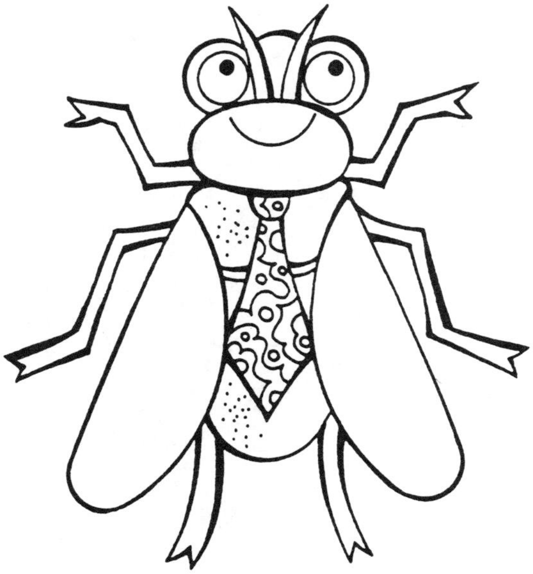

Did you ever see a fly, wearing a tie . . .

7

Did you ever see a bear combing his hair . . .

8

Did you ever see llamas eating their pajamas . . .

9

Did you ever have a time, when you couldn't make a rhyme . . .

10

Song 3

Brush Your Teeth

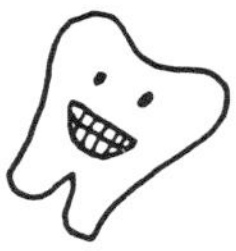

Use this song with these themes:

Dental Health

My Body

Rote Counting

Telling Time

Rhyming

Materials to be used with these activities:

Toothbrush

Toothpaste

Paper

Crayons

Scissors

Contact Paper or Laminate

Shoe Box

Toiletry Items (see page 4)

Storybook *Dr. de Soto*

About This Song

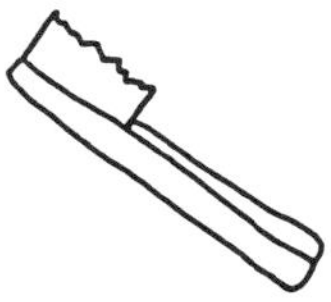

Traditional
Adapted by Raffi & Louise Dain Cullen

Brush Your Teeth is a great "reminder" song for young children. It is a lot of fun to hear someone sing you a song, rather than ordering or demanding that you go brush your teeth. Show the children how you can actually sing part of the chorus as you brush your teeth – "ch ch ch chuh, ch ch ch ch chuh."

Use this song as part of a dental health unit as well as using it for many other educational topics, such as: telling time, fractions, rote counting, and rhyming.

Brush Your Teeth

Adapted and arranged by Louise Dain and Raffi

Moderately Bright

2. When you wake up in the morning and it's quarter to two,
   And you want to find something to do, *Chorus*
3. When you wake up in the morning and it's quarter to three,
   And your mind starts humming twiddle de dee , *Chorus*
4. When you wake up in the morning and it's quarter to four,
   And you think you hear a knock on your door, *Chorus*

Taking Care of Myself

The objective for this activity is for the children to learn ways that they can take care of themselves. This can be accomplished by creating a "touch-and-tell box" that the children can use to identify objects and tell their purpose or function. Children love this activity because it is "mysterious." They never get to look in the box – they only get to feel the objects inside.

This is a wonderful activity for increasing the child's ability to name objects, answer questions, name body parts, tell or retell a story, follow directions, and to be able to sequence events.

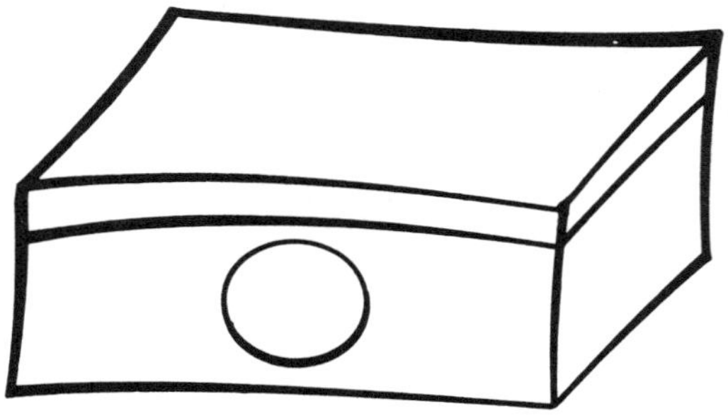

Directions for creating the Touch-and-Tell box: You will need a cardboard box (a shoebox will work well), masking tape, contact paper, sharp scissors or knife (to be used with adult supervision or by the adult). Tape the box closed with masking tape. Cover the box with contact paper. Cut a hole about three-inches in diameter – large enough for a child to put one hand through the hole. Fill the box with a variety of items.

What to put in the box: Fill the box with various toiletry items, such as a toothbrush, toothpaste, washcloth, soap, comb, brush, tissue, shampoo, etc.

Place the items in the touch-and-tell box. Ask each child to reach in the box and tell you what he/she feels. Have the child pull the object out of the box to see if she/he was correct. Ask the children to describe how you would use the object.

It is a lot of fun to sing Raffi's song, *Brush Your Teeth*, after you play this game. You can also write new lyrics for this song by adding lines about other good health habits, such as replacing the line, "Brush your teeth," with, "comb your hair," "wash your hands," or "get your rest."

Healthy Teeth

To complete this activity you will need the story book, *Dr. de Soto* by William Steig. It is a funny story about a very small dentist who sees a very large and possibly "dangerous" patient: the sly fox!

Read the story and have the children discuss what dental problem the sly fox had and why it caused his tooth to hurt. Talk about the effect the following have on teeth: eating too much sugar, brushing regularly, flossing regularly, drinking milk, eating vegetables, visiting the dentist twice a year, biting hard candy, etc.

Brush Your Teeth

This activity has several different visuals that you and the children can make together. First, you will need to reproduce the large "teeth and smile pattern" at the bottom of this page. Color the smile and laminate, or cover with clear contact paper, for durability.

On page 16 you will find teeth brushing sequence cards. Copy these cards, color, cut out and laminate for durability. You will also need a real toothbrush and toothpaste.

Show the children the toothbrush and toothpaste. Ask them what it is used for and why they think it is so important to remember to brush their teeth. Show the children the sequence cards and have them tell you the sequence as you put the cards in order. Do the actions of brushing your teeth using the toothbrush with toothpaste on the laminated "teeth and smile pattern."

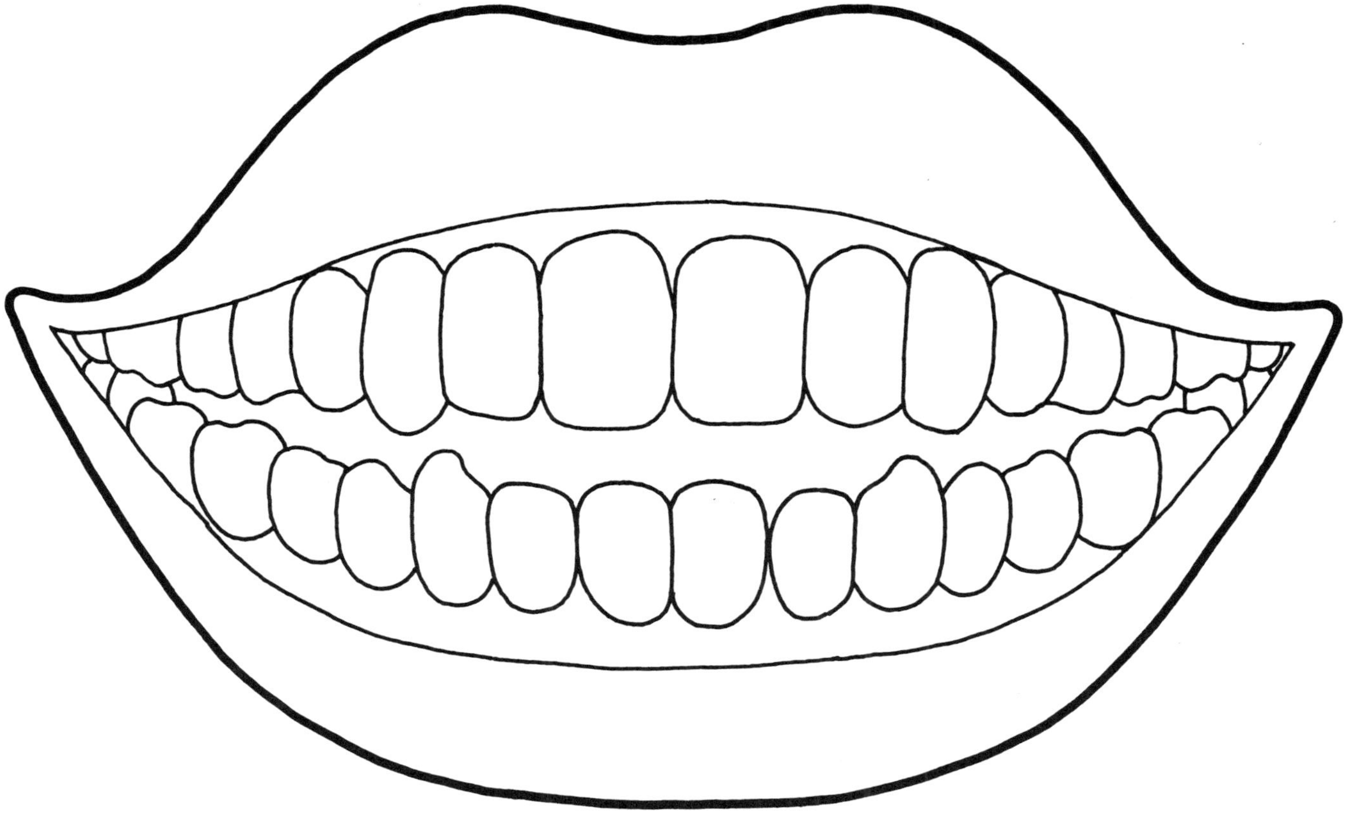

Toothbrush Rhyme

I jiggle the toothbrush again and again.	(pretend brush teeth)
I scrub all my teeth for awhile.	
I swozzle the water to rinse, and then	(puff out cheeks to swish)
I look at myself and I smile.	(big smile)

Sequence Cards

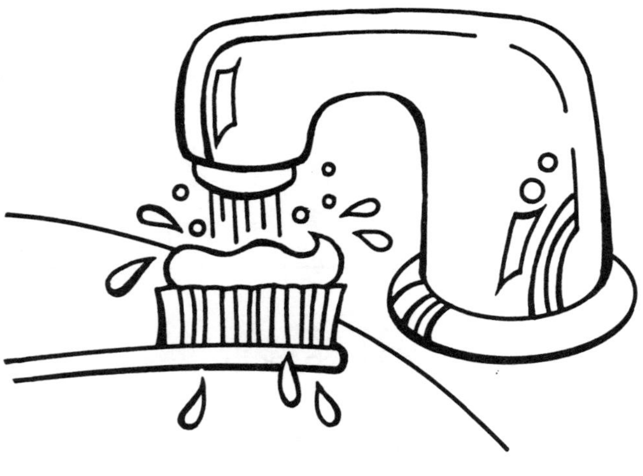

Song 4

Robin In The Rain

Use this song with these themes:

Birds

Spring

Animals

Weather

Materials to be used with these activities:

Recipe Items (see page 18)

Flannel Board

Felt

Glue

Paper

Pencils

Tagboard

Toilet Paper Tubes

Yarn

Pine Cones

Peanut Butter

Milk Cartons

Bird Seed

About This Song

From Scissors & Songs, Book 2 by Claire Senior Burke.

Robin In The Rain is a delightful song to teach! As you sing the song, the descriptive vocabulary will enable the children to feel the personality and emotions of the Robin. Some of the words and phrases may be new to the children: "saucy, nimble, socks of yellow." Help the children to understand the meanings of these words.

Use this song to help the children understand inferences through sentence starters and open-ended questions, such as: Why are the worms wishing the robins will stay at home?; Why do you think robins like the rain? and; Think of reasons why rain is so important.

Robin In The Rain

Words and music by Claire Senior Burke

"Myself In The Rain" Storybook

On page 20, you will find the reproducible page for the small, four-page storybook, Myself in the Rain. To complete this activity, the children should first sing the song, *Robin In The Rain,* and discuss some of the things that robins like to do when it rains. Then have the children discuss some of the things that they like to do when it rains.

Read the pages of the reproducible story to the children. Page 1 is the cover of the book. Page 2 reads, "Here I am in my raincoat." Page 3 reads, "This is my umbrella." Page 4 reads, "Here I am with my best friend jumping in a rain puddle." The children create illustrations to go with each of the sentences. When the children are finished drawing and coloring, fold the booklet according to the directions printed in the page.

Rain, Rain, Go Away

Using felt make an umbrella and at least 10 raindrops to be used on the flannel board. (Magnetic strips can also be used so that the objects adhere on a refrigerator or other metal surface.) Have the children place the raindrops, OVER, UNDER, ON and BELOW the umbrella.

Recite the nursery rhyme, *Rain, Rain Go Away.* Discuss the types of clothing that should be worn outside on a rainy day.

Rainy Days

Have the children draw a picture of a "cloudy day." Be sure to tell the children not to draw any raindrops on their pictures. The picture is just to be of a cloudy day.

Once the pictures are completed, tell them that they are now going to be able to turn their "cloudy days" into "rainy days." They can do this by putting drops of white glue on their pictures. When the glue dries it will be clear and look like raindrops.

To add extra fun to this project, draw a robin in the picture and label the painting *"Robin In The Rain."*

I'm A Doll

Encourage the children to make paper dolls of themselves. This can be accomplished by simply drawing a figure on a piece of tagboard, or you can make a "real" looking paper doll by adding a photograph of the child's face onto the figure. Children enjoy creating a paper doll that "really" looks like them.

Then make an outfit for each season that the doll can wear. Include tabs on the clothes so that they will stay on the doll.

Cold Weather Pine Cone Bird Feeders

In the song, *Robin In The Rain,* the children learned how robins hunt for worms after a rain. There are times when birds have a difficult time finding food, especially if they live in a cold northern climate. Children can help the birds by building bird feeders during the winter months. Each child will need a pine cone, peanut butter, bird seed or bread crumbs, sticks or spoons for spreading the peanut butter, string and paper clips for hanging the pine cone bird feeder.

1. Tie the string around the pine cone.
2. Spread the peanut butter over the pine cone.
3. Roll the covered cone in birdseed or bread crumbs.
4. Hang the pine cone outside, near a window, so the children can observe the birds eating the crumbs or birdseed.

Warm Weather Bird Feeders

This is a simple bird feeder that uses recycled materials, such as milk cartons. You may use either a large half gallon milk carton or the small lunch-size milk cartons.

Help the children cut large square sections out of the sides of the milk carton. Attach a string from the top so that the bird feeder can be hung. Fill with birdseed and enjoy watching your feathered friends.

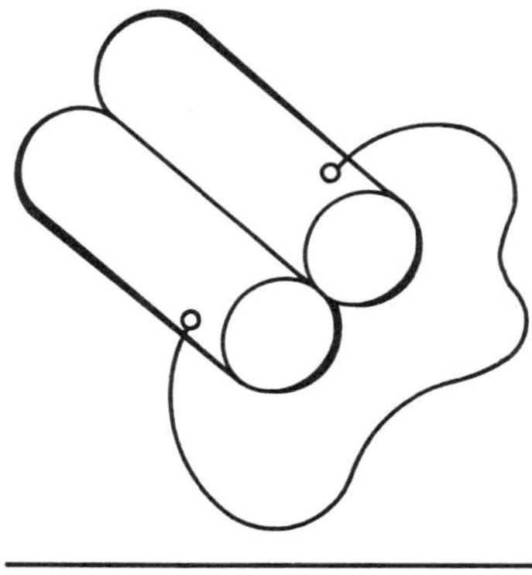

Bird Watching

Make a list of the most common types of birds that are found in your area. Make a pair of binoculars and go on a bird watch.

Staple together two toilet paper roll tubes (see illustration). Attach a string so the "binoculars" can be worn around the neck. Go outside and keep a record of how many different types of birds you can find. Did you see any robins?

Sing a New Song

Robin In The Rain is a fun song to sing. Make up a song of your own by substituting the names of different animals. For example, Tiger in the rain, what a noisy fellow. Tiger in the rain, with his stripes of yellow. Running through the jungle, swift and fast and sleek. Roaring for his dinner, he wants a plate of meat. Tiger in the rain, he doesn't like the weather, etc.

fold #1

fold #2

1.

Myself In The Rain Story

by ____________

2.

Here I am in my raincoat.

3.

This is my umbrella.

4.

Here I am with my best friend jumping in a rain puddle.

Song 5

Five Little Frogs

Use this song with these themes:

Frogs

Amphibians

Counting

Subtraction

❖❖❖❖❖❖❖❖❖❖

Materials to be used with these activities:

Flannel Board or Magnetic Board

Paper

Crayons

"Real" Tadpoles

Contact Paper or Laminate

String or Yarn

About This Song

Words and music by Louise B. Scott & Virginia Pavelko.
Copyright © 1954 Bowmar Publishing (ASCAP)

Children love frogs! There is something exciting about watching a frog jump, listening to a frog "croak," and holding a squirmy frog! As children sing the song, *Five Little Frogs,* they will enjoy pantomiming the "subtraction" story of the song. Begin with five children (or as many children as there are verses that you would like to sing). Line the children up on their "speckled log." The children can mimic the actions of the frogs in the song. What a fun way to introduce the mathematical concept of subtraction!

(Use the pattern found on page 24 when the children dramatize this song.)

Five Little Frogs

Unaccompanied, easy going tempo

Words and music by
Louise B. Scott & Virginia Pavelko

Next verse: Four frogs, then Three, Two, One, "No green speckled frogs".

Leap Frog

Leap frog is a traditional game of childhood. It is a game played with friends. Remember the first time that you jumped over the back of a friend? It was exciting! Teach the young children in your life the game of leap frog. Sing the song, *Five Little Frogs,* as you play the game.

How Do Frogs Grow?

Discuss with the children the stages of development in the life of a frog. Find photographs of these stages to show the children. Make up a sequencing game for the children to play. Enlarge the illustrations. Copy, color, laminate and cut apart the polliwog-to-frog sequence illustrations. Back the pictures with felt, sandpaper, or self-stick velcro for the flannel board. You can also use self-stick magnetic tape for a magnetic board (or to stick to the refrigerator door).

Real Frogs In My House!

It is a fun adventure to collect polliwogs or tadpoles from a pond. Put them in an large container with the original pond water and let the children enjoy watching them grow into frogs. The container should be emptied everyday and replaced with fresh pond water. This will provide natural food for the tadpoles.You may supplement with tiny amounts of goldfish food if needed. If you are unable to provide good living conditions for the tadpoles you should return them to their natural environment.

As soon as the tadpoles have reached maturity *(and you have real frogs living at your house)* please return them to the pond where you found them! You can make the experience of returning the frogs a special learning experience for the children. All animals thrive best when they are allowed to live in their natural habitats!

Five Polliwogs

Five polliwogs swam near the shore.
The first one said, "I have been this way before."
The second one said, "I have a funny tail."
The third one said, " And a tail can help me sail."
The fourth one said, " My legs are getting strong."
The fifth one said, "It will not be very long."
The five polliwogs deep in the bog,
Gave three croaks and each one became a frog.

(Discuss with the children how a polliwog turns into a frog. Show the children pictures of the various stages of development.)

Frog Life Cycle Big Book

Enlarge the following illustrations. Have the child create a five-page big book on the life cycle of a frog. The child should draw each life cycle stage on a single piece of paper. Print or dictate a sentence about each illustration.

Punch holes on the left side of each page and tie the pages together with yarn to form a book. *(You may wish to reproduce the following illustrations to give the child a good idea of what each of the life cycle stages looks like.)*

Eggs

Tadpole

Tadpole with hind legs

Tadpole with front legs

Frog

Frog Character Prop

Copy this pattern for each child. The child can color and cut out the pattern. String a piece of yarn on the top of the frog and then let the child wear the frog like a necklace. The children will love wearing their frogs as they sing *Five Little Frogs.*

Song 6

I Wonder If I'm Growing

Use this song with these themes:

My Body

Growth

Nutrition

Family

Self-Esteem

Materials to be used with these activities:

Pictures of Babies

Variety of Items Needed to Care for a Baby (see page 26)

Dolls

Paint

About This Song

Music by Raffi.
Words by Raffi, Deborah Pike, Bonnie Simpson, and Bert Simpson

I Wonder If I'm Growing captures a child's feelings on wanting to be "bigger," and talks of the ways that parents nurture and encourage growth in their children.

I Wonder If I'm Growing

As much as children want to grow-up, they are also enchanted with stories about when they were babies. The activities found on this page help children realize how much they have grown and how much they have learned to do since they were babies.

Let's Learn About Babies

Guide the children through a discussion about babies. Show the children pictures of babies found in magazines or books. Find out how much the children understand about babies and have them share their ideas about taking care of babies.

- Can new babies walk or crawl? How do they get around?
- What kinds of food do you think babies should eat?
- How do babies tell us what they want? Do they talk?
- Babies cry! Why do you think babies cry? What are they trying to tell us?
- What kinds of toys are good for babies?
- Do you remember when you were a baby?
- What kinds of things did you like to do when you were a baby?
- Do you have a baby brother or sister? Can you tell us about the things that the baby in your home does?

What Do Babies Need

Prepare a box filled with some of the things that are used in caring for a baby. If you are not a parent, or do not have access to baby things, ask some of the parents to help provide you with the following items:

- Bottle
- Pacifier
- Diaper
- Blanket
- Stroller
- Baby Powder
- Infant Seat
- Baby Food Jar
- Formula
- Diaper Bag
- Stuffed Animal
- Rubber Pants
- Newborn Outfit
- Baby Washcloth
- Crib Mobile
- Baby Spoon
- Baby Wipes
- Rattle
- Music Box
- Baby Booties

Show the children the items one at a time. Ask the children what the item is and why it is needed. Also talk about high chairs, cribs, play pens, mechanical swings, and car seats. It is astounding all the equipment that a tiny baby needs. A young child's response to all the equipment can be even more astounding!

Caring For Baby

After the first two activities, the children should have a pretty good idea of all the things that are needed to take care of a baby. Not only do babies need a lot of equipment, but they need a lot of time! Have the children role play ways they would care for a baby. Use dolls for the role playing – bathing, feeding, rocking, talking, and of course, singing to baby!

As a group, have the children create a lullaby that they would like to sing to their dolls.

Let's Be Babies

Talk about the ways that infants learn to move. First they wiggle, turn over, lay on their backs or stomachs with their heads up, kick their feet, bat with their hands, crawl, pull themselves up to a standing position, walk, and finally run. Have the young children imitate the movement of a baby. Look at how much they have grown and how much they have learned.

Make Yourself Big

People come in all different sizes. Children are small, adults are tall. Some children can be tall, while some adults can be small. Let the children pretend that they are people that come in many different sizes. Have the children stretch, crouch, spread arms and legs while following these directions.

- ❖ Make yourself tall.
- ❖ Make yourself taller.
- ❖ Make yourself wide.
- ❖ Make yourself wider.
- ❖ Make yourself small.
- ❖ Make yourself smaller.
- ❖ Make yourself big.
- ❖ Make yourself bigger.
- ❖ Make yourself short.
- ❖ Make yourself shorter.
- ❖ Make yourself long.
- ❖ Make yourself longer.

I Am Getting Bigger

Have the children share baby pictures of themselves. They will enjoy seeing what their friends looked like as babies. Talk to the children about how much they have grown. What are some things that they can do now that they could not do as a baby? Weigh and measure the children. Mark the children's heights on the wall. Mark how tall a baby would be in inches or centimeters. The children will be impressed when they see how much they have grown!

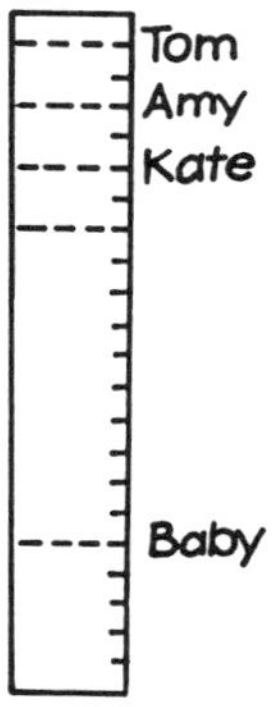

Little Baby

Here is a baby so soft and small *put up baby*
His/Her legs can't walk, so he/she must crawl.
He/she drinks from a bottle and naps in a crib. *put up bottle*
He/she dribbles his/her food, so he/she wears a bib. *put up bib*
When his/her pants are wet, he/she starts to cry.
His/her mom/dad will change them, so he'll/she'll be dry. *put up diaper*

(The instructor or parent repeats the rhyme and encourages the children to join him/her. Enlarge the illustrations for the flannel board or magnetic board.)

These are my little handprints
Because I am so small.
But soon my hands will grow,
And I will be very tall.

My Handprints

Song 7

Aikendrum

Use this song with these themes:

Make-Believe

Memory Skills

Nutrition

Space

❖❖❖❖❖❖❖❖❖❖

Materials to be used with these activities:

Self-Stick Velcro

Yarn

Lids from Pots & Pans

Coffee Can

Comb

Wax Paper

Sequins, Ribbons (Various items from a Craft Box)

Recipe Items (see pages 30 & 31)

Old Magazines

About This Song

Traditional

Aikendrum is a great make-believe song that can be used to stimulate creativity. Have you ever heard of a man living in the moon? What do you think he looks like? If you could rewrite this song using your favorite foods, what would Aikendrum look like?

You can use the song *Aikendrum* to teach children about proper nutrition and the food pyramid. Ask them to write verses when Akiendrum is only made with fruits or vegetables, or breads, or dairy products.

March Tempo

Aikendrum

Traditional

2. And he played upon a ladle, a ladle, a ladle,
   He played upon a ladle and his name was Aikendrum.
3. And his hair was made of spaghetti...
4. And his eyes were made of meatballs...
5. And he played upon a ladle...
6. And his nose was made of cheese...
7. And his mouth was made of pizza...
8. And he played upon a ladle...
9. There was a man lived in the moon...

Build Aikendrum & Sing-Along

Copy, color, and laminate all of Aikendrum's facial feature patterns found on page 32. Add a piece of self-stick velcro to the back of each of the pieces. Use a yellow piece of yarn for the outline of the moon.

Using a flannel board, wrap the yellow yarn in a circle. As you sing, add the correct "food" facial feature. The children will delight in watching Aikendrum's face appear as you sing the song.

The Aikendrum Marching Band

Aikendrum is a terrific song to be sung while the children form a marching band. Use objects that can easily be found in a classroom or home. Frying pan lids make wonderful cymbals, wooden spoons turn into rhythm sticks, soup spoons make a great clanging sound, coffee cans can be bass drums, and wax paper over the teeth of a comb makes an instant harmonica. Play, sing, and march!

You may wish to create some of the instruments in the section *Old MacDonald Had A Band,* found on pages 78 and 79.

My Own Aikendrum

The song Aikendrum can provide a great art experience. Allow the children the freedom to create their own Aikendrum by using materials left on a table. Be sure that you have a wide variety to chose from. Here are some good suggestions: scrap fabric, rick-rack, ribbon, yarn, thread, sequins, glitter, buttons, markers, construction paper, crayons, glue, scissors, or anything that you have readily on-hand. You will be delighted with how many different Aikendrums there will be. Make one yourself!

Let's Gobble Up An Aikendrum Snack

Children love to cook and prepare special snacks. Here is a healthy *Aikendrum* recipe that is fun to prepare. It utilizes many healthy foods, is easy to make, and is a snack that children will eat!

Let each child spread cream cheese or peanut butter on a rice cake, round bread, or toast cut into large circles. Provide the children with carrot circles, banana slices, raisins, sliced strawberries, celery, or any other healthy food that you believe will work in creating an edible Aikendrum!

Aikendrum For Everybody

Aikendrum is all about a man – not a woman – in the moon. Like many traditional songs now enjoyed by children, it was written well before we became aware of the important role inclusive language plays in a child's social, emotional, and linguistic development.

The children will delight in changing the word *man* to woman, grandma, mom, teacher, girl, boy, etc. The children will have fun visualizing all sorts of different people in the moon.

Aikendrum Lunch

Children love assisting in the kitchen! Here is a fun lunch recipe that can be used to reinforce the concept of good nutrition and can be used to create the face of Aikendrum on a pizza!

You will need: refrigerated biscuit dough; pizza sauce; shredded mozzarella cheese; and various toppings, such as: mushrooms, celery, carrots, onions, green peppers, and assorted other vegetables.

What you do:

1. Separate the biscuit dough. Give one biscuit to each child to flatten into the shape of a pizza.
2. The children can help prepare the vegetables.
3. Each child may spoon on their own pizza sauce and sprinkle the cheese on his or her pizza.
4. Each child tops his or her own pizza with individual choices of cheese and vegetables. Encourage the children to make their pizza look like Aikendrum.
5. Bake at 375° until the biscuit dough browns and serve warm.

Paper Plate Meals

Let the children look through discarded magazines or old coloring books. Cut out pictures of various foods. Have the children paste the foods on paper plates according to appropriate "healthy" meals.

These plates make fun additions to the "housekeeping corner" or a child's play house area.

Use these patterns with the "Build Aikendrum & Sing-Along" activity found on page 30.

Song 8

Bumping Up And Down

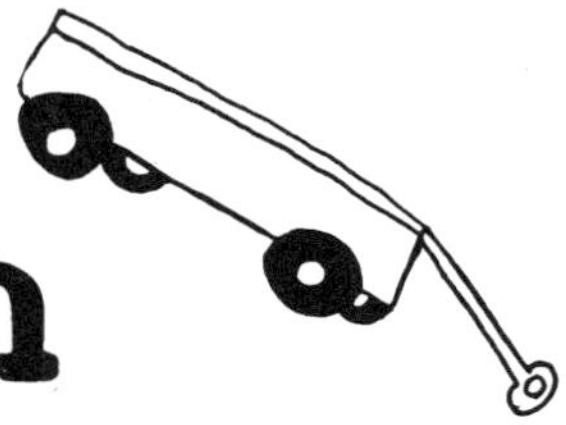

Use this song with these themes:

Positional Concepts

Simple Machines

Tools

Transportation

Materials to be used with these activities:

Wagon

Tools & Nails

Wood Scraps

Washboard

New Pencils

Shoe Boxes

Construction Paper

Paper Punch

Magazines

Obstacle Course Items (see page 35)

About This Song

Traditional

Bounce up and down as you sing this favorite traditional children's song, *Bumping Up and Down.* The children will giggle as they pretend to ride in the wiggley old red wagon, delight as they pantomime pretending to fix the wagon's broken wheel, and they will want to sing this song over and over and over again! It's one of those songs that children never get tired of singing.

Bumping Up And Down

Quick with a bounce

Traditional
Adapted by
Raffi and Ken Whiteley

2. One wheel off and the axle's broken...
3. Freddie's gonna fix it with his hammar...
4. Bumping up and down in my little red wagon...
5. One wheel off and the axle's broken...
6. Laura's gonna fix it with her pliers...
7. Bumping up and down in my little red wagon...

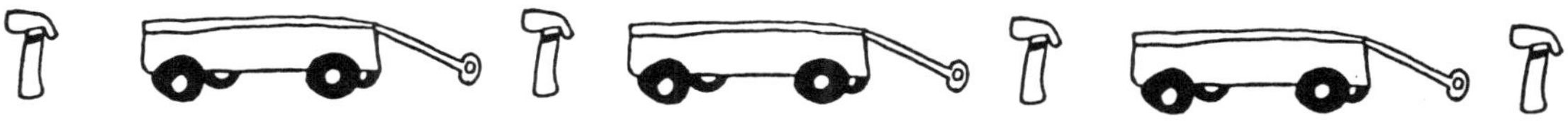

Six Simple Machines

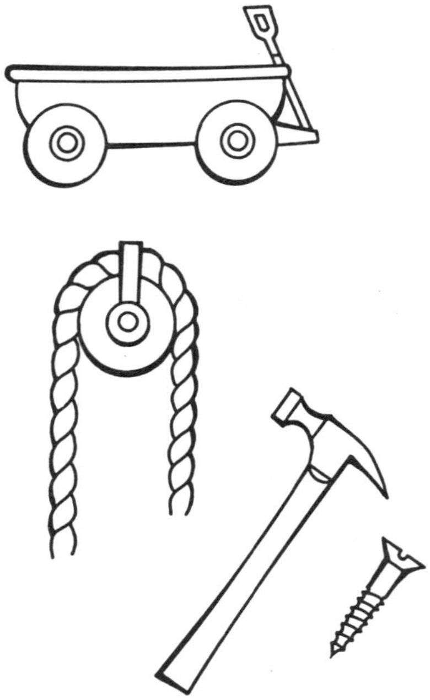

A unit on simple machines provides a perfect opportunity to teach the song *Bumping Up and Down.*

The red wagon in the song is an excellent example of a piece of equipment that utilizes many of the basic machine principles. The red wagon has ***wheels and axles*** for motion. The handle could work as a ***lever***. The wagon could be pulled up an ***incline plane*** with a ***pulley***. If you wanted to park the wagon on a hill, you could place a ***wedge*** under the tire so it would not slide back down the hill. Also, if you look carefully, I'm sure that you would find some ***screws*** holding the wagon together.

Children love to experiment with "tools." Provide the children with wood, hammers, nails, etc. You will be surprised with the incredible creations that even very young children can make with only small pieces of wood, a hammer, and nails.

The Kitchen Washboard Band

If you listen carefully to the music on Raffi's recording of *Bumping Up and Down*, you will hear a washboard, jug, guitar, and harmonica. Many young children will not know what a washboard is or what it was once used for. Locate one and tell the children some history about washboards, and then demonstrate how a washboard is played. Do the same thing with a jug. The children will marvel at the sounds these "old time" instruments can make. Let the children play-along as you sing!

Bumping Up and Down in My Little Red WHAT?

Bumping Up and Down is a wonderful song to use when you are encouraging children to create their own verses. Tell the children that you are going to be singing the song, but this time the children will get to say what type of vehicle they wish to drive and then they must tell how it is broken.

Here is an example that you can sing to the children, and then let them create their own verses:

Bumping up and down in my giant red space ship.
Bumping up and down in my giant red space ship.
Bumping up and down in my giant red space ship.
Won't you be my darlin'?

No more fuel and the engine's broken.
No more fuel and the engine's broken.
No more fuel and the engine's broken.
Won't you be my darlin'?

I'm going to fix it with my laser
I'm going to fix it with my laser
I'm going to fix it with my laser
Won't you be my darlin'?

My Own Wagon

Ask each of the children to bring a shoe box to school. Paint the shoe box red, or any other color that the children might enjoy.

The parent or teacher should put four holes in the box. These holes should be located where the wagon wheel axle would be located. Using new, unsharpened pencils, push them through the holes.

Cut out four cardboard wheels. Punch a hole with a paper punch in the center of the wheels. Push the wheels onto the axle. Gently push the wagon so the children will be able to see the movement of the wheels on the wagon.

For extra fun: Let the children cut out of construction paper a small hammer and pliers that the children can keep in their wagons. When you sing the song, the children can actually pull a wheel off the wagon and use their tools (which are handy if you keep them in the wagon), enabling them to be ready to fix their wagon when it comes to that part of the song.

Up and Down

The positional concepts of up and down are two of the easiest concepts for children to learn. Children experiment with these concepts from the time that they are very little. For example, "pick me up," "put me down." Climbing up and down on the furniture and playground equipment also helps children understand these concepts.

Children are generally able to act out or physically move to an up or down position. It is more difficult for a child to look at a picture or at another person, and identify and name the position. For example, "Where is the bird?" Response: "The bird is up in the tree." Let the children practice at naming the position from looking at pictures in magazines and books or from telling you the location of children at a playground.

This is a fun activity on a flannel board. Make a felt tree and felt birds. The birds can fly UP, DOWN, AROUND, HIGH, LOW, ON, OFF, NEXT TO, BELOW, ABOVE. The possibilities are endless, as well as the experience for enriching vocabulary.

Create an Up and Down Obstacle Course

Children love obstacle courses. Design your own obstacle course by using hoola hoops, chairs, jump ropes, blankets, tables, blocks, etc.

Run through the obstacle course and then try it backwards!

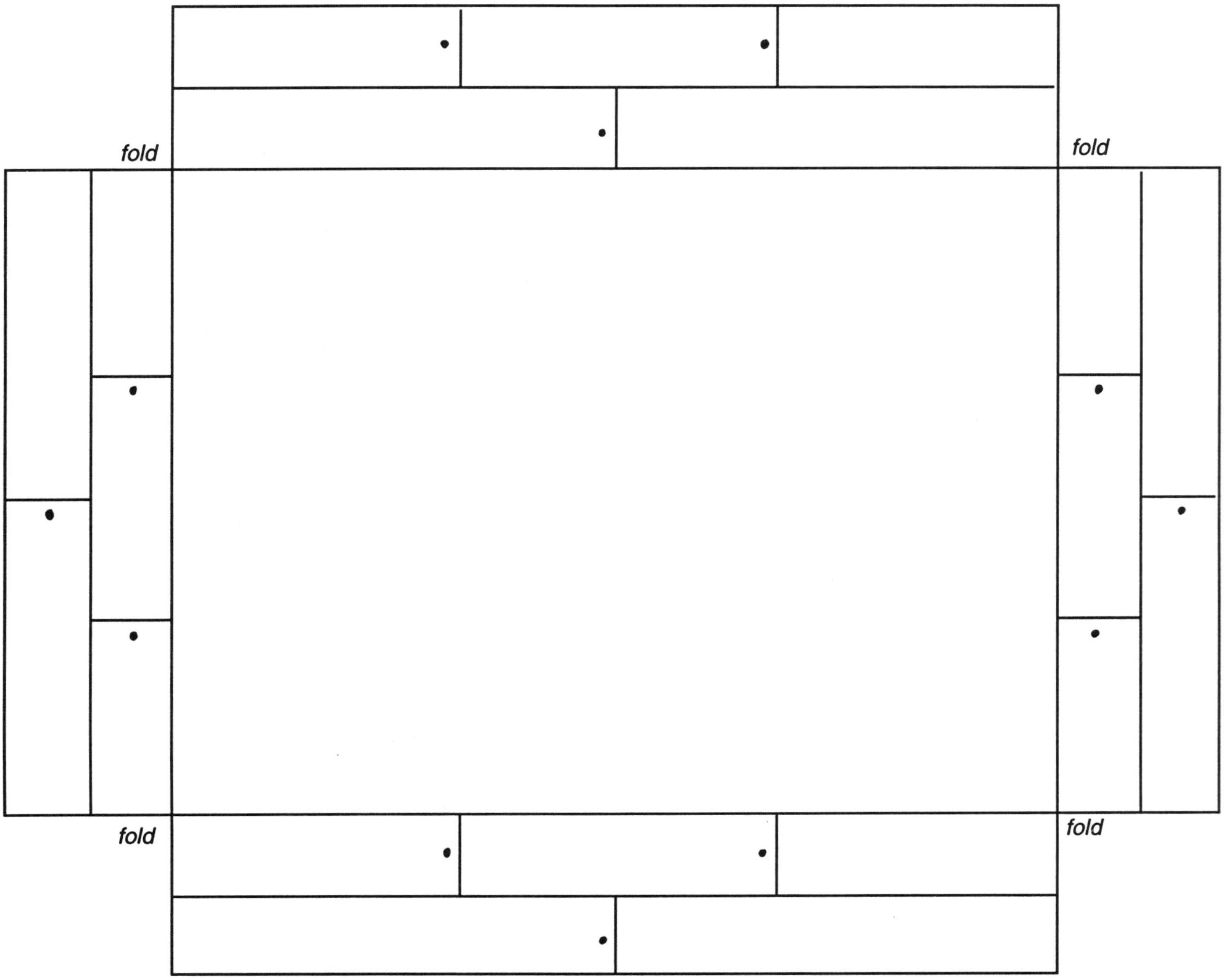

Cut out wagon. Color it red. Fold up the sides and tape together. Cut out wheels and tape or paste to the side of the wagon. Add a pipe cleaner handle.

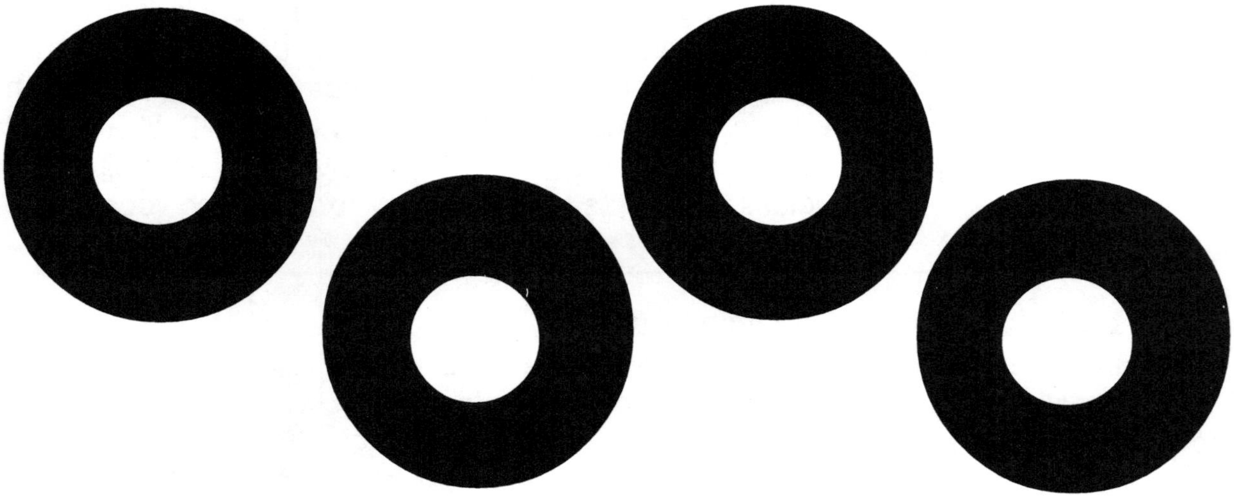

Song 9 Must Be Santa

Use this song with these themes:

Christmas

Make-Believe

Colors

Auditory Memory Skills

Sequencing

Materials to be used with these activities:

Red Construction Paper

White Crayon

Large Marshmallow

Apple

Toothpicks

Raisins

Powder Puff

Cotton

Paper

Santa Hat

Crayons

Brads

About This Song

Words and music by Hal Moore & Bill Fredericks.
TRO Copyright © 1960 Hollis Music, Inc. (BMI)
New York, NY. Used by permission.

Must Be Santa is an exciting song for children to sing – it anticipates the arrival of Santa Claus, and enables the children to sequence all the verses. Each verse builds upon the next. This song will quickly become a seasonal favorite!

2. Who's got boots and a suit of red?
Santa's got...
Who wears a long cap on his head?
Santa wears...
Cap on head, suit that's red,
Special night, beard that's white,
Chorus

3. Who's got a great big cherry nose?
Santa's got...
Who laughs this way, "Ho, ho, ho?"
Santa laughs...
Ho, ho, ho, cherry nose,
Cap on head, suit that's red,
Special night, beard that's white,
Chorus

4. Who very soon will come our way?
Santa very...
Eight little reindeer pull his sleigh,
Santa's little...
Reindeer sleigh, come our way,
Ho, ho, ho, cherry nose,
Cap on head, suit that's red,
Special night, beard that's white,
Chorus twice

Star Santa

Here is a wonderful old story that is similar to the song, *Must Be Santa*. In the song, the children sing descriptions of Santa, while in the story, the children must listen, follow directions, and create a Santa. Give each of your children a red construction paper star and a white crayon. Have them create as you read this short story.

Many years ago a story was told about a star that wanted to fall down to the earth and make the children happy. He did fall - down, down, down. A fat jolly gentleman picked him up and said, "I will have a pattern of you made for all the boys and girls."

Mrs. Claus made the pattern, cutting it out of red paper. The children used their white crayon and made a face on one of the points, arms and legs on the other points and a belt across the middle. The star Santa hung on the Christmas tree and made all the children happy.

Apple Santa Claus

This is an easy project that makes a fitting centerpiece for a holiday table or as a holiday decoration.

Use a large, whole apple for the body. Attach a marshmallow to the top, with a toothpick, for the head. Press raisins into the marshmallow for the eyes, nose, mouth and ears. Press cotton under the marshmallow for the beard.

Felt Pin Santa

This is a wonderful gift idea for mom or dad, grandma or grandpa, or a special friend.

Use a powder puff for Santa's head. Cut Santa's cap, eyes, mouth, and nose out of felt and glue these to the powder puff. Glue cotton for a beard. Attach a safety pin to the back of the powder puff. The children will be proud to give this pin as a gift.

A Letter To Santa

Let the child dictate a letter to Santa Claus, either orally or on tape. Send a response back to the child written from Santa. How exciting to actually get a letter from Santa. "It must be Santa, Santa Claus!"

A "Must Be Santa" Game to Play

Divide the children into groups of eight to ten. Each group stands in a straight line. Give a "Santa" hat to the child first in line. When the music starts (either the recording of *Must Be Santa* or the children singing the song), he or she must place the hat on the head of the next child. Each child places the hat quickly on the head of the child next to her/him. When the hat gets to the last person, it is started back in the opposite direction. The child holding the hat when the music is stopped is out of the game. Continue until only one child remains.

When all the groups have finished playing, the winners in each group may compete against each other. The last child standing wins the game.

My Special Friend

I have a special friend: he's as jolly as can be. You can guess who he is if you play along with me. In the center of the paper, draw a circle:

Step 1:

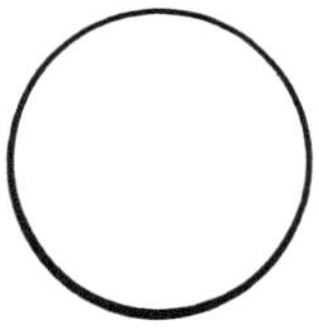

Draw a smaller circle for a mouth that says "Ho, ho, ho!"

Step 2:

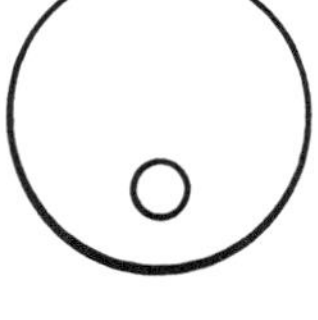

Above the mouth place a cute red nose and white mustache.

Step 3:

To this face add the eyes that sparkle ever so bright.

Step 4:

On top of his head draw a red hat with white trim.

Step 5:

Have you guessed that it's Santa Claus! It really is him!

Santa Claus

Here is the chimney	(make fist, enclose thumb)
Here is the top	(place palm on top of fist)
Open the lid,	(remove top hand)
And out Santa will pop.	(pop up thumb)

Directions:
Make a copy for each child.
Let the children color and cut out the parts.
Attach legs with brads.

Song 10

Willoughby Wallaby Woo

Use this song with these themes:

Names

Rhyming

Self-Esteem

❖❖❖❖❖❖❖❖❖❖

Materials to be used with these activities:

Parachute

Flashlight

Large Paper

Crayons

Paper Punch

Tape Recorder

Cardboard

Construction Paper

Markers

String

About This Song

Willoughby Wallaby Woo has become a traditional song for all children to learn during their early years. It provides a wonderful activity for teaching rhyming, or to be used as a name game during circle time, or for just having fun!

Children love hearing their own names in a song. Use the children's names in your class, or the names of their family members. Watch the children's eyes light up when you sing "Willoughby wallaby rad, an elephant sat on dad. Willoughby wallaby llama, an elephant sat on mama!"

Willoughby Wallaby Woo

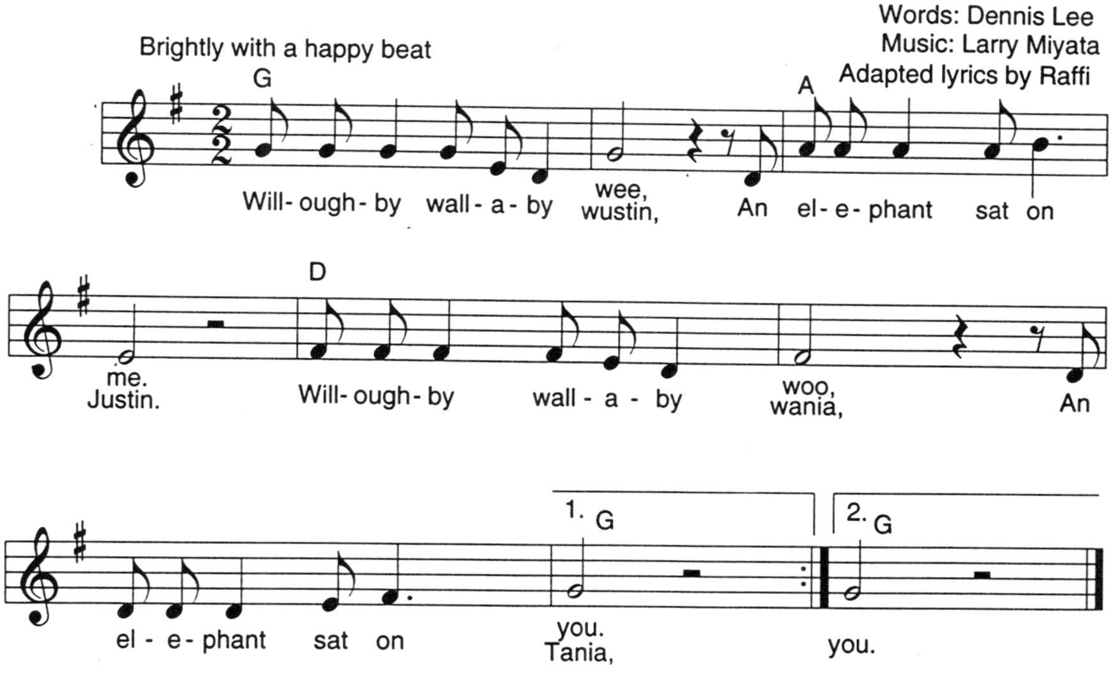

Parachute Movement

Willoughby Wallaby Woo is a great song to use with a parachute. Have a group of children stand in a circle holding the edge of the parachute. As you sing this song use the names of the children in your group. Each time a child hears their name in the song, that child will run under the parachute and then run back to their place. The children can pretend that the parachute is the elephant. So when the elephant sits on them, the light airy feeling of the parachute will be the elephant.

Children love music, they love movement, and they love being the center of attention. This activity has all three of those "favorites!"

Shadow Dancing

Shine a light behind the children as they stand in front of a blank wall. They will be able to see their shadows against the wall. They can pretend that they are the elephant in the song *Willoughby Wallaby Woo.* Have the children clasp their hands together, hold their arms straight, and bend over. Show the children how to swing their arms like an elephant's trunk. The children will enjoy watching their elephant shadows move and dance.

How Many Animals Can Willoughby Wallaby Woo?

Every verse in the song *Willoughby Wallaby Woo,* includes an elephant who is sitting on somebody. Let the children have the fun of rewriting this song. In every line change the animal and the way the animal moves. This makes the song a little more difficult. Here is an example: Willoughby Wallaby Woo, a tiger pounced on you, Willoughby Waby Watie, a snake crawled up on Katie, etc."

Children can be extremely clever with the words and images that they create. Let the children draw a picture of each new line that they create. Punch holes along the side and turn it into a *Big Book of Willoughby Wallaby Woo (our own version).*

I'm Thinking

Children love guessing games. Before you sing each line of the song with a child's name, let the children guess who should be in the song. State a few descriptive sentences and see if the children can guess who you are talking about.

I Love Making Music

Willoughby Wallaby Woo has a section of music in the middle of the song where Raffi sings along to the melody of the music with nonsense syllables–for example "rat tat tat tat tat tat – la la la la la la la, etc.

Let the children make a recording of their own using rhythm instruments and nonsense syllables. Let each child choose an instrument and create their own sound that they would like to sing. To make your recording, have each child sing their own verse, and end the song with the grand finale of everyone singing together! You will have a musical hit on your hands!

Look At Me - I'm On T.V.

A cut out of a television screen is a wonderful prop to have in a classroom for many reasons. It can be used to increase a child's verbal skills, self-expression, self-confidence, as well as using it for a creative play prop.

As you sing *Willoughby Wallaby Woo,* the child whose name you are singing can jump up and run and "be on television."

Here is how you can make the television. Use a large piece of cardboard and cut out the center. Decorate the front so it looks like a television screen. Add knobs and buttons. Hang the television somewhere in your learning environment where the children can stand behind the screen.

Let's Move!

Early childhood is a time for constant movement. It is nearly impossible for a young child to stay still for very long. It is incorrect to think that small children should stay still for long periods of time. So much learning happens when children are active! Let the children practice all the various movements that they can name: gallop, run, skip, hop, jump, crawl, walk, etc.

Sing *Willoughby Wallaby Woo*. Change the movement of the elephant. Here are some examples:

Willoughby Wallaby Woo, an elephant runs with you.
Willoughby Wallaby Wee, an elephant crawls with me.
Willoughby Wallaby Woo, an elephant jumps with you.
Willoughby Wallaby Wee, an elephant gallops with me.
Willoughby Wallaby Woo, an elephant walks with you.
Willoughby Wallaby Wee, an elephant skips with me.
Willoughby Wallaby Woo, an elephant rolls with you.

The children perform the actions as they sing the words.

Elephant Pattern.

The children will enjoy making their own elephant stick puppet that they can use when they sing *Willoughby Wallaby Woo*. Copy, color, cutout and attach a tongue depressor or craft stick.

Song 11

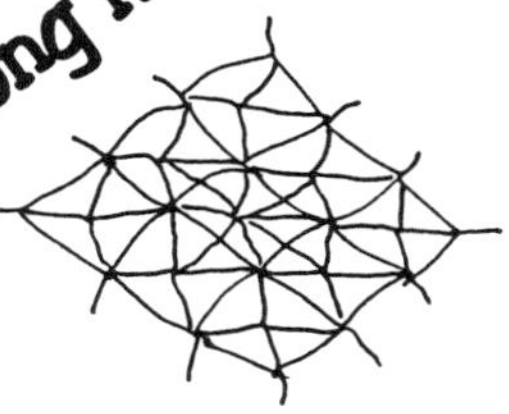

Spider On The Floor

Use this song with these themes:

- Spiders
- Body Parts
- Self-Esteem
- Rhyming

Materials to be used with these activities:

- Large Paper Plates
- Small Paper Plates
- Black Yarn
- Styrofoam Ball
- Pipecleaners
- Construction Paper
- Black Spray paint
- Oatmeal Box
- Screen
- Hand Mirror

About This Song

Words and music by Bill Russell

Spider On The Floor is a circle story – a story that winds itself around until it ends up back at the beginning. The spider begins on the floor, and ends up back on the floor. The predictability of the story makes it safe, even though there is a spider crawling on you! This song is destined to become a favorite! Another fun idea is to use Raffi's Book, *Songs to Read™ – Spider On The Floor.* It's delightful and full of surprises!

Spider On The Floor

Unaccompanied with freedom

Words and music by Bill Russell

Modulate up a semitone with each verse for six verses.
Spoken phrase after verse 6. Verse 7 in original key.

2. Now the spiders's on my leg, on my leg.
   Oh, the spider's on my leg, on my leg.
   Oh, he's really big! This old spider on my leg.
   There's a spider on my leg, on my leg.

3. Now the spider's on my stomach, on my stomach.
   Oh, the spider's on my stomach, on my stomach.
   Oh, he's just a dumb old lummok,
   this old spider on my stomach.
   There's a spider on my stomach, on my stomach.

4. Now the spider's on my neck, on my neck,
   Oh, the spider's on my neck, on my neck.
   Oh, I'm gonna be a wreck, I've got a spider on my neck.
   There's a spider on my neck, on my neck.

5. Now the spider's on my face, on my face,
   Oh, the spider's on my face, on my face.
   Oh, what a big disgrace, I've got a spider on my face.
   There's a spider on my face, on my face.

6. Now the spider's on my head, on my head,
   Oh, the spider's on my head, on my head.
   Oh, I wish that I were dead, I've got a spider on my head.
   There's a spider on my head, on my head.

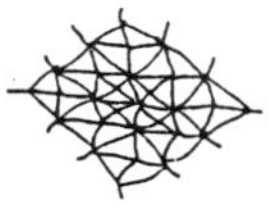

Spoken: But he jumps off.

7. Repeat 1st. Verse.

My Own Spider On The Floor

Make your very own spider that you can keep on the floor of your room. Use two paper plates – a dinner size plate for the body and a dessert-size plate for the head. Overlap the two plates slightly and staple together. Paint both sides of the plates black.

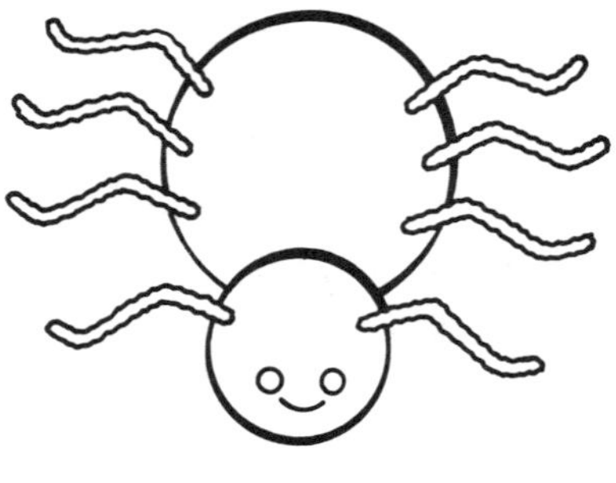

Punch four holes on each side of the body. Punch two more holes at the "neck" of the spider. Insert a pipe cleaner in each pair of punched holes, and bend to look like legs. Thread black yarn through the holes in the neck so that the spider can be hung up. Glue small white pom-poms or plastic moveable eyes on the head.

Chubby Spiders

These spiders are easy-to-make. Spray paint (black) 4-inch styrofoam balls. The child can give their spiders legs by inserting eight pipe cleaners into the ball. Glue on construction paper eyes and a mouth. Moveable eyes are a nice extra touch!

Sing In A Circle

Children will begin to understand the concept of a circle story if your "sing" or "tell" the story in a circle.

You will need as many people as there are verses in the song (6 verses: floor, leg, stomach, neck, face, head). Use one of the spiders you have made or a stuffed animal. The first child puts the spider on the floor. When the next verse begins, the second child picks up the spider and puts it on her/his leg. The third child puts the spider on his/her stomach and so on.

Finally, when you reach the last verse, the child who is holding the spider on her/his head will end the song by tossing the spider to the child who began the song when the lyrics say, "But he jumps off. . etc."

Even if you are teaching in a large classroom setting, you can divide your class into groups of six children. All the groups can play "sing in a circle" at the same time.

Creepy Crawler Catcher

You will need: an oatmeal box, screen or netting, heavy tape, scissors, and string.

What you do: Cut out windows in the box. Securely tape the screen or netting to the inside of the box. Punch a hole on each side and attach a string for a handle. Take the children on an exploratory adventure and let them try to find some "creatures" for their creepy crawler catcher. Free the animals when you are done observing them!

Look At Me

Spider On The Floor is a wonderful song for helping young children learn to identify and name their body parts. Here are some fun suggestions:

1. Stand in front of a floor length mirror and have the child dentify body parts by pointing to the image in the mirror.
2. Using a hand mirror, tell the child to identify parts of their head and face that are reflected in the mirror.
3. Cover half of a large mirror with paper. Ask the child to stand directly before it and tell what parts of their body are not reflected in the mirror.

Naming Our Body Parts

The children sit or stand facing the teacher or parent, who asks them to name body parts as he/she touches them: head, neck, arms, elbows, wrists, thumbs, fingers, trunk, hips, legs, thighs, knees, ankles, feet, toes, hair, eyes, ears, nose, mouth cheek, chin, eyebrows, eyelashes, etc. Pair the children off and use one child as the teacher and the partner as the responder. Alternate the partners in these roles.

Another fun version of this activity is for the parent or teacher to say, "There's a spider on your chin!" And the child would touch her/his chin. "There's a spider on your elbow!" And the child should touch her/his elbow. Adding the element of the spider makes for a lot of fun!

Using Our Body Parts

Have the children lie on the floor, far enough apart so that their hands do not touch when outstretched. The children should lie with their feet together, looking at the ceiling, with their hands alongside their body. Ask the children to relax and not look at you. Then lead them in the exercises, doing them slowly.

Do not use the words "left" or "right" with preschool, kindergarten or even first grade children. Instead use a reference point in the room, such as "the leg next to the door," "the arm nearest the window," etc.

Here are some examples:

1. Drag the hand by the door along the ground until it is over your head.
2. Raise your hands as high as they can go.
3. Move your leg that is nearest to the window.
4. Move your leg that is nearest to the door.
5. Raise up both of your legs.

Make two sets of cards. Let the children play lotto or a memory matching game.

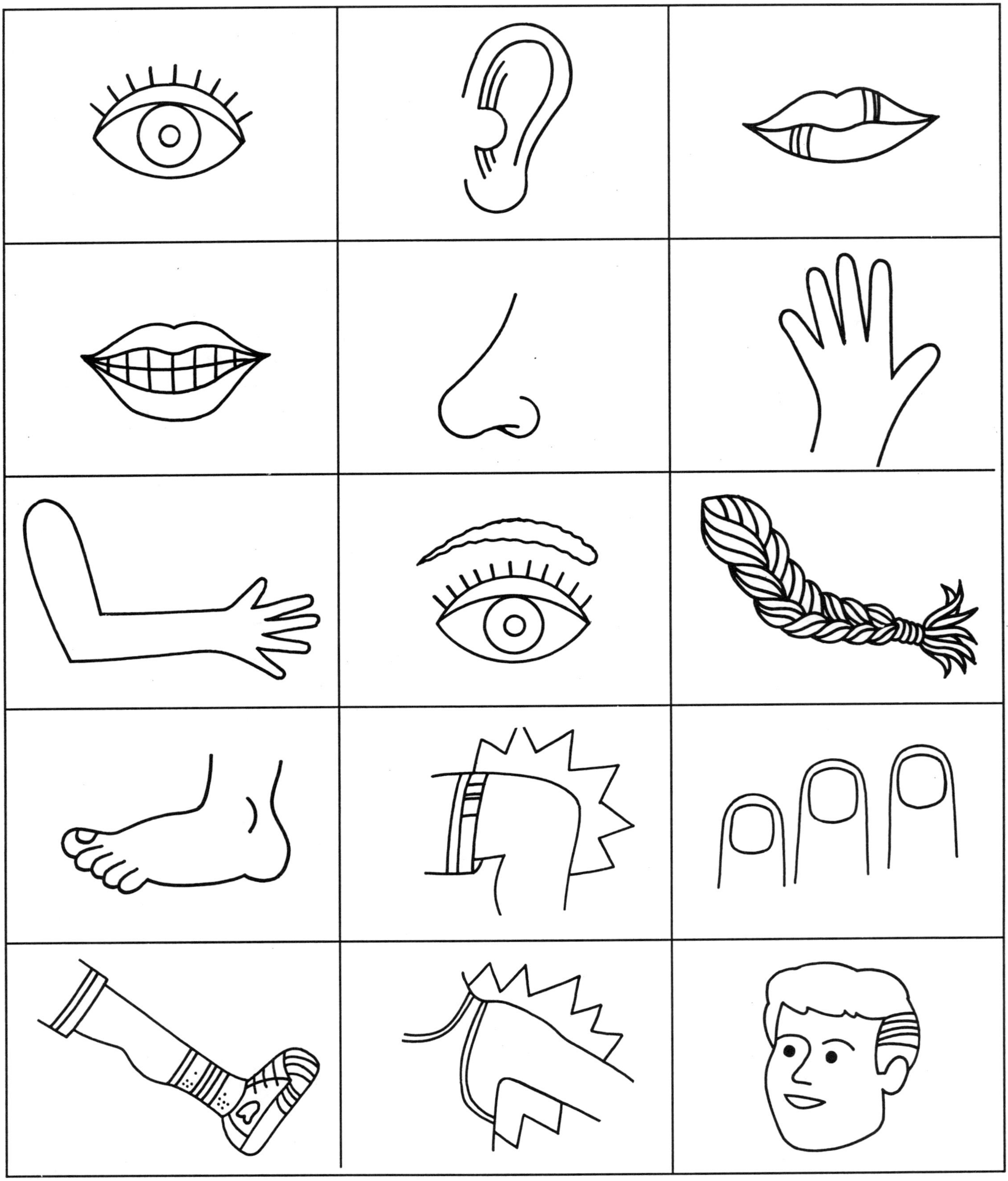

Song 12

Baa Baa Black Sheep

Use this song with these themes:

The Farm

Pets

Colors

Counting

Nursery Rhymes

◆◆◆◆◆◆◆◆◆◆

Materials to be used with these activities:

Poster Board

Nursery Rhyme Pictures

Scissors

Brad/Glue

Paper Punch

Yarn/Scissors

Drama Box Items (see page 51)

Cotton

Paper Towel Tube

Tape Recorder

About This Song

Traditional

Copyright © 1976 Homeland Publishing (CAPAC)

Baa Baa Black Sheep is a traditional nursery rhyme set to music. Raffi sings the song beautifully, almost like a lullaby. Have the children sing this song "quietly." Can they sing in a whisper?

This is also a fun song to use when you are teaching colors. Raffi sings about a black sheep and a white sheep. Use the sheep pattern on page 52 to make a variety of colored sheep. Now you can sing about the "red sheep" or the "green sheep."

Baa Baa Black Sheep

Gently

Traditional

Mother Goose Wheel

Nursery rhymes are an essential part of early childhood. *Humpty Dumpty, Jack & Jill, Baa Baa Black Sheep,* and so many others help children to increase language skills. Here is a fun prop to make that you and the children will enjoy.

Cut out three poster board circles as shown. The first and third circles should be the same size; the middle one should be cut one inch larger in diameter.

Divide the large wheel into six equal sections. Draw a circle in each section, and in that circle paste a nursery rhyme picture. On the first wheel cut out a circular window that matches the pictures on the middle wheel. On the back of the third wheel, make an easel stand as shown. Attach all three circle with a brad.

To play the game, the child should spin the middle wheel. The child must then recite the nursery rhyme that appears in the window.

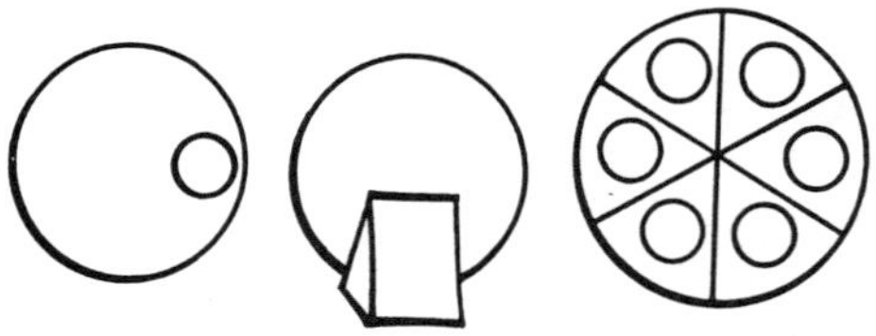

My Baa Baa Black Sheep Book

Sing the song with the children. Create a big book of this rhyme. Have the children illustrate on poster board each line of the song. Include a cover. Punch holes in the sides and tie together in book form. The children will love to "read and sing" this song.

Another fun idea is to let the children change the verses of the song. When you get to the section that says, "One for my master, one for my dame, one for the little boy . . ." Let the children decide who the three people are that would get their wool. Draw three pictures and staple together in book form.

Mother Goose Character Poster Cards

This activity will take some extra effort, but it will be well worth it! Once you have created these character poster cards you will have them for years to come.

On each sheet of poster board, draw a character. (You can create the Black Sheep, Little Miss Muffet, or you can use any of the other characters found in any of the songs on Raffi's *Singable Songs.)*

This activity can be used with any story, song, or rhyme. Cut out a hole for the face and the hands. Color or paint the character poster cards.

To use the poster cards, have one child "wear" the poster by allowing his/her face to show through the face opening, and placing his/her hands through the hand openings. The child can now dramatize the story or song.

Character poster cards are wonderful for language development. Young children can hold the posters and invent their own stories and songs.

Baa Baa White Sheep

As you listen to the rhyme *Baa Baa Black Sheep*, you will notice that Raffi sings a second verse of Baa Baa White Sheep. On page 52, you will find an outline of a sheep. Make copies for the children. Let the children "paint" glue with a brush over the sheep and press on cotton balls

The sheep really will be "soft" to touch!

The Drama Box

Keep a collection of small objects that relate in some manner to the nursery rhymes. For example, you could have a pie tin for "Little Jack Horner" or "Four and Twenty Black Birds." A stuffed animal sheep would make a nice prop for "Baa, Baa Black Sheep," "Mary Had A Little Lamb," or "Little Boy Blue."

Hats, aprons, jackets, shoes, scarves, and belts always make reciting a rhyme, or singing a song, more fun! These types of activities promote the development of self-esteem and increase language skills.

How Many Ways Can You Sing?

Raffi sings *Baa Baa Black Sheep* softly. Try singing *Baa Baa Black Sheep* just like Raffi. How did you do? Now try singing the song a new way. Can you sing it fast? Can you sing it slow? Can you sing it loud? Can you sing it soft?

Try humming the song. Next try performing the song with a kazoo. Here is an easy, make-it-yourself kazoo.

Each child will need a paper towel tube. Help the children punch a hole in one end of the cardboard tube. Seal the other end of the tube with wax paper and a rubber band. The children should then hum into the open end.

Our Own Musical Recording

Children love hearing themselves on a tape recorder. Make your own cassette tape of as many nursery rhyme songs as the children are able to sing.

Practice the songs before you attempt to record. Add rhythm instruments, such as the kazoo from the above activity, and any other extra touches that you can think of. Besides Raffi's music, this tape will quickly become a favorite!

The activity for this pattern,
Baa Baa White Sheep, is found on page 51,

Song 13

Going To The Zoo

Use this song with these themes:

Zoo Animals

Field Trips

Gross Motor Skills

Dramatics

❖❖❖❖❖❖❖❖❖❖

Materials to be used with these activities:

Animal Pictures (see page 56)

Pellon or Sandpaper

Crayons

Scissors

Glue

Tagboard

Paper Punch

Yarn

About This Song

Words and music by Tom Paxton.

Zoo animals are always an exciting unit to teach. Young children (even toddlers!) delight in learning about animals: how they move, how they feel, how they sound, what they eat, and how they live and care for their babies.

In the song, *Going To the Zoo*, children can pretend that they are at the zoo. The children will enjoy making props and costumes to sing with this song. Use a headband and let the children attach construction paper "ears," (elephant ears, lion ears, tiger ears, etc.). The children will also enjoy creating their own original verses for this song.

Going To The Zoo

2. Look at all the monkeys swinging in the trees,
   Swinging in the trees, swinging in the trees.
   Look at all the monkeys swinging in the trees,
   We can stay all day.
   Chorus
3. Look at all the crocodiles swimming in the water,
   Swimming in the water, Swimming in the water.
   Look at all the crocodiles swimming in the water,
   We can stay all day.
   Chorus
4. Repeat 1st. verse.
   Chorus twice

Zoo Animal Concentration

You will need a set of zoo animal pictures pasted on identically sized cards. You may choose to use either two cards of each animal or four cards of each animal. Patterns for these cards are found on page 56. Lay the cards face down on the table top. Have the children take turns turning over two cards at a time. If the child finds a matching set they may keep the cards. If the animals do not match, the child must turn the cards back over on the table.

Concentration is a wonderful game for developing memory skills. Play this game throughout the year using a variety of pictures.

Mixed-Up Zoo Animals

Find pictures of zoo animals. You may wish to draw your own is you are artistic. Tracing animals from library books also works well, as does using pictures from old coloring books.

Once you have a collection of animal pictures, cut the animals out and then cut off their heads. Glue a piece of self-stick velcro or sandpaper on the back of all the bodies and heads. They can now be used on a flannel board. (Use magnetic tape on the back and the pieces will work on a refrigerator or magnetic board.)

Mix up the animal parts. Ask the children to locate the correct pieces and rebuild all the animals as they should be. This is a fun way to teach animal name identification.

Another idea: Let the children create "nonsense animals." For example, an elephant's head and a monkey's body. What would you name this new animal? How about a monkeyphant? Use the new animals that you have created when you sing, *Going To The Zoo.* Who can create the silliest animal? How many nonsense animals can you come up with?

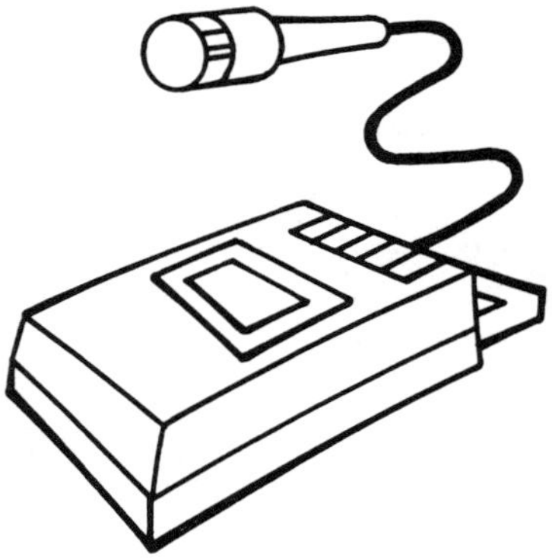

Near and Far Zoo Animal Noises

Use a record player or a tape recorder. Turn the volume up and down to demonstrate the concept of noises that are near and noises that are far away.

To make this activity even more fun, have the children make a tape recording of zoo animal noises. Play the tape for the children. Turn the volume up and down. Tell the children that you are sitting in the jungle. Can you hear all the animals? Can you tell which of the animals are nearby and which of the animals are far away?

My Zoo Animal Book

Let the children brainstorm a list of animals that they could see in a zoo. From that list let the children dictate a short paragraph about each animal. When you write this information, use one page per animal. Encourage the children to use the knowledge that they have already acquired about the animals. You will be surprised at how much information young children will be able to provide you. Write the sentences exactly as the children say them.

After the paragraphs are completed the children can make an illustration for each of the animals. Glue each animal paragraph and picture on a single page. Punch all the pages with holes and put together in book form. Have the children draw covers for their books on construction paper. (A note of caution: This project should take several days to complete. Preferably, one animal per day. The children will become bored and work too fast if they think they must complete the entire project in one day.) The children will really enjoy "reading" their books. Let the children look up the animals in the song, *Going to the Zoo.* Sing the song using the animals in their books.

We Do As The Animals Do

Pantomime the movements of the animals in the song, *Going To The Zoo.* Here are some additional movement ideas that the children will think are a great deal of fun:

- How does an elephant move when he is taking a bath?
- How does a giraffe move when he is eating?
- How does a monkey move when he is scared?
- How does a hippo move when he is tired?
- How does a snake move when he is in a hurry?
- How does a lion move when he is prowling at night?
- How does a seal move when he is performing on stage?

The Animals Escaped From the Zoo

News flash! All the animals have escaped from the zoo! We must find them! Hide pictures or toy animals around the room. Send the children on a search to find the animals. Help those children that are having a difficult time finding the animals. Make sure that every child has at least one animal when the search is over.

After the children have found all the animals, have the children sing, *Going To The Zoo,* with a new twist:

We're going to the zoo, zoo, zoo
How about you, you, you?
You can come too, too, too
We're going to the zoo, zoo, zoo.

We're bringing back the _______, feed them please!
The _______ are back, take good care of them please!

Song 14

My Dreydel

About This Song

Written by S.S. Grossman & S.E. Goldfarb.

Many years ago, when the Jewish people first began celebrating Hanukkah, the rabbis set the laws for Hanukkah, but it was the people who created the fun holiday traditions, such as the Dreydel game. The game originated because it was not practical to work with candles as the only light source, but it was possible to play games.

The Dreydel game has a great importance in Jewish history. When the ruler Antiochus forbade people to study the Torah, children secretly memorized the Torah. When these children would get together to study what they had memorized, they always brought "tops" of clay with them. When Syrian soldiers approached, the children would quickly take out their tops and begin playing. The soldiers never knew that the children were actually studying the Torah.

My Dreydel

Written by S.S. Grossman & S.E. Goldfarb

Unaccompanied

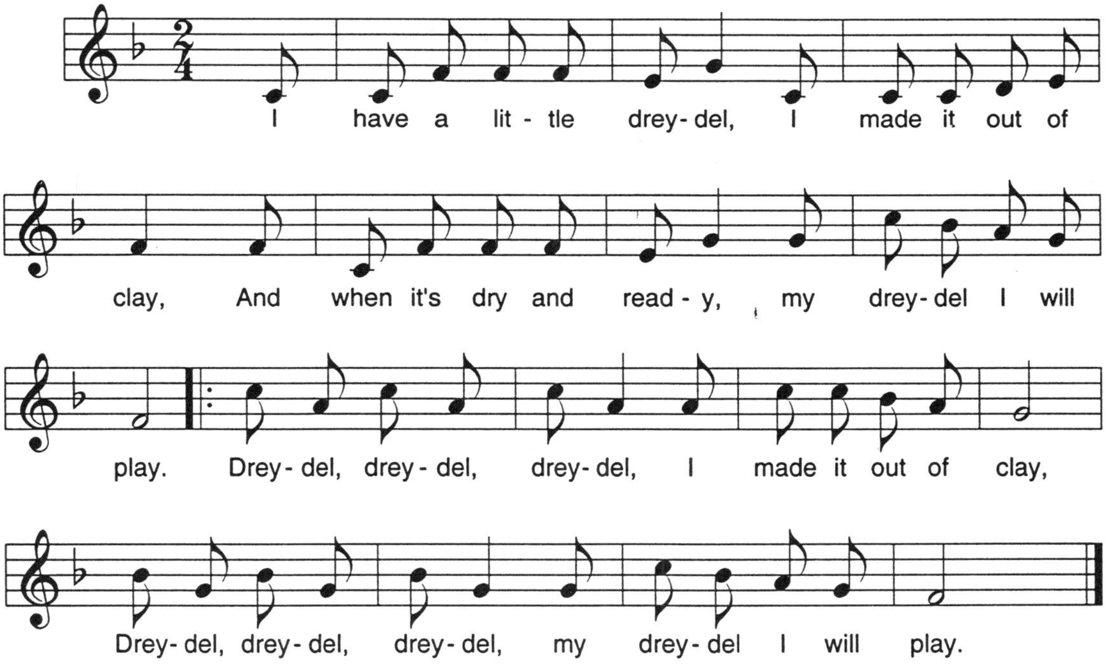

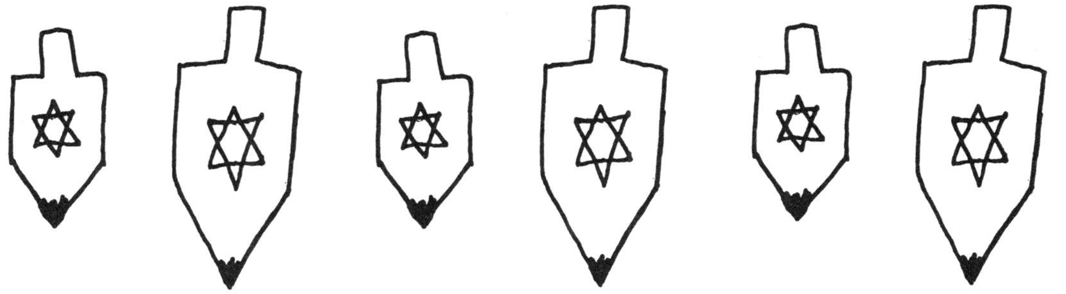

Use this song with these themes:

Hanukkah

Games

Counting

Taking Turns

Materials to be used with these activities:

Recipe Items (see page 58)

Gold & Blue Crayons

Paper

Scissors

Margarine or Coffee Can Plastic Lids

Exacto Knife (only to be used by an adult)

Paint

Sponges

Card Stock

Tape

Pencils

Latkes

Latkes are a traditional Hanukkah food that most children love to eat. If your children have never tasted latkes, they will enjoy making them as well as eating them.

What you need: 4 medium potatoes that are peeled and grated; 1 teaspoon (5 ml) grated onion; 2 teaspoons (10 ml) flour; 2 well-beaten eggs; 1/2 teaspoon (2.5 ml) salt; vegetable oil; frying pan; spoon; and, spatula.

What you do: Mix all the ingredients together. The batter should be smooth but heavy. If the mixture seems too dry add another egg. Heat the oil in the frying pan and drop spoonfuls of the batter into the oil. Fry over medium heat until brown on the bottom. Turn and brown the other side. Drain on paper towels. Serve with applesauce.

Dreydel Chant

This is a fun chant to learn. Say the chant as you are playing the Dreydel game (directions for the game are found on page 59). After you have sung the song *My Dreydel*, learn the chant and what each of the letters means.

Nun, gimmel, hey, shin
Dreydel spin, Dreydel spin.
Nun, gimmel, hey, shin
Will I win? Will I win?

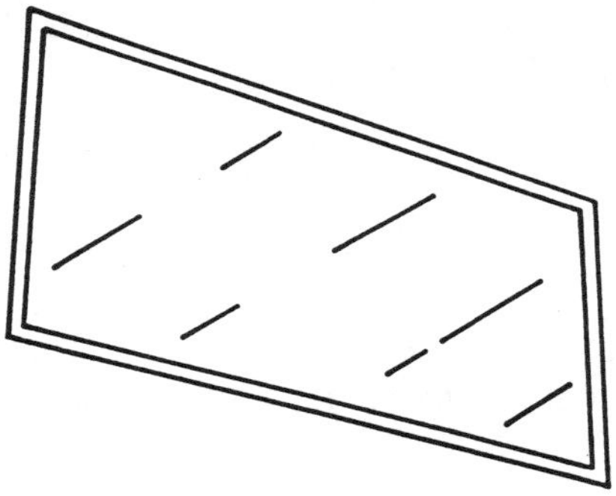

Blue and Gold

Various colors are associated with different holidays and traditions. For example, red and green are colors associated with Christmas. People who celebrate Hanukkah often think of the colors blue and gold. Have your children make Hanukkah placemats using these colors. The placemats may be colored with crayons, or collage placemats can be made from used wrapping paper.

Hanukkah Cards

Prepare several stencil patterns ahead of time. An easy way to create a good stencil is to use discarded plastic lids from coffee or margarine containers. An adult cuts out the shape in the center of the plastic lid with an exacto knife. Stencils can also be made out of cardboard. The pictures on the right will provide you with some ideas. Have the children sponge paint of the stencils to decorate their cards, then let the cards dry.

The children will especially enjoy this project if you mail their cards to someone special.

Dreydel #1

Make copies of Dreydel pattern #1, found on page 60, on cardstock. Give one to each child. Instruct the children to color the four triangles that contain the symbols. Suggest that they use four different colors. This will make it easier for them to identify each symbol. Have them cut out the Dreydel. Make a hole in the center and insert a straw cut in thirds. Spin the Dreydel and it will rest on one of the four sides. This is the side which they must identify in order to play the game.

Dreydel #2

Make copies of Dreydel pattern #2, found on page 60, on cardstock. Give one to each child. Instruct the children to color the four squares that contain the symbols. They may use four different colors for easier identification of the symbols. They should cut out the pattern and punch holes in the center of the two X's. Fold on the lines to make a box, keeping the symbols on the outside. Tape the necessary edges. Put a sharpened pencil through the two X's. Spin the Dreydel and play accordingly.

Symbols on the Dreydel

נ	– NUN	– take nothing
ג	– GIMMEL	– take all
ה	– HEY	– take half
ש	– SHIN	– give one

How To Play The Dreydel Game

Everyone should choose something that they would like to play with – pennies, stickers, checkers, etc. Take a small group of these objects and put them in front of you. Each player takes a turn spinning the Dreydel. Follow the directions on the symbols of the Dreydel. Players who have nothing left are out of the game. The player with the most objects is the winner.

Picture Chart

If a child has two coins and the pot has 2 coins

Then:

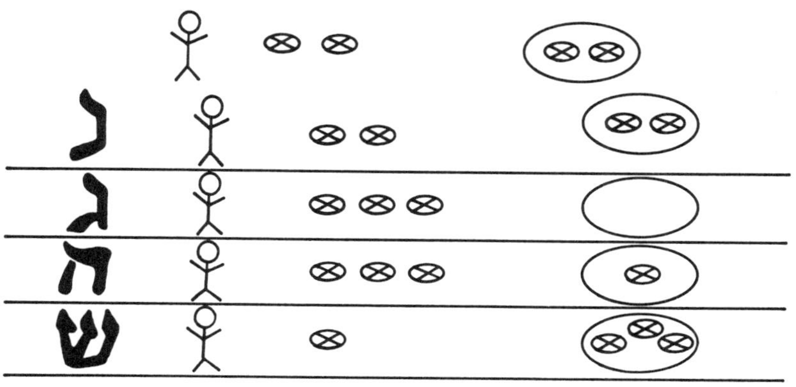

Dreydel Patterns

Dreydel #1

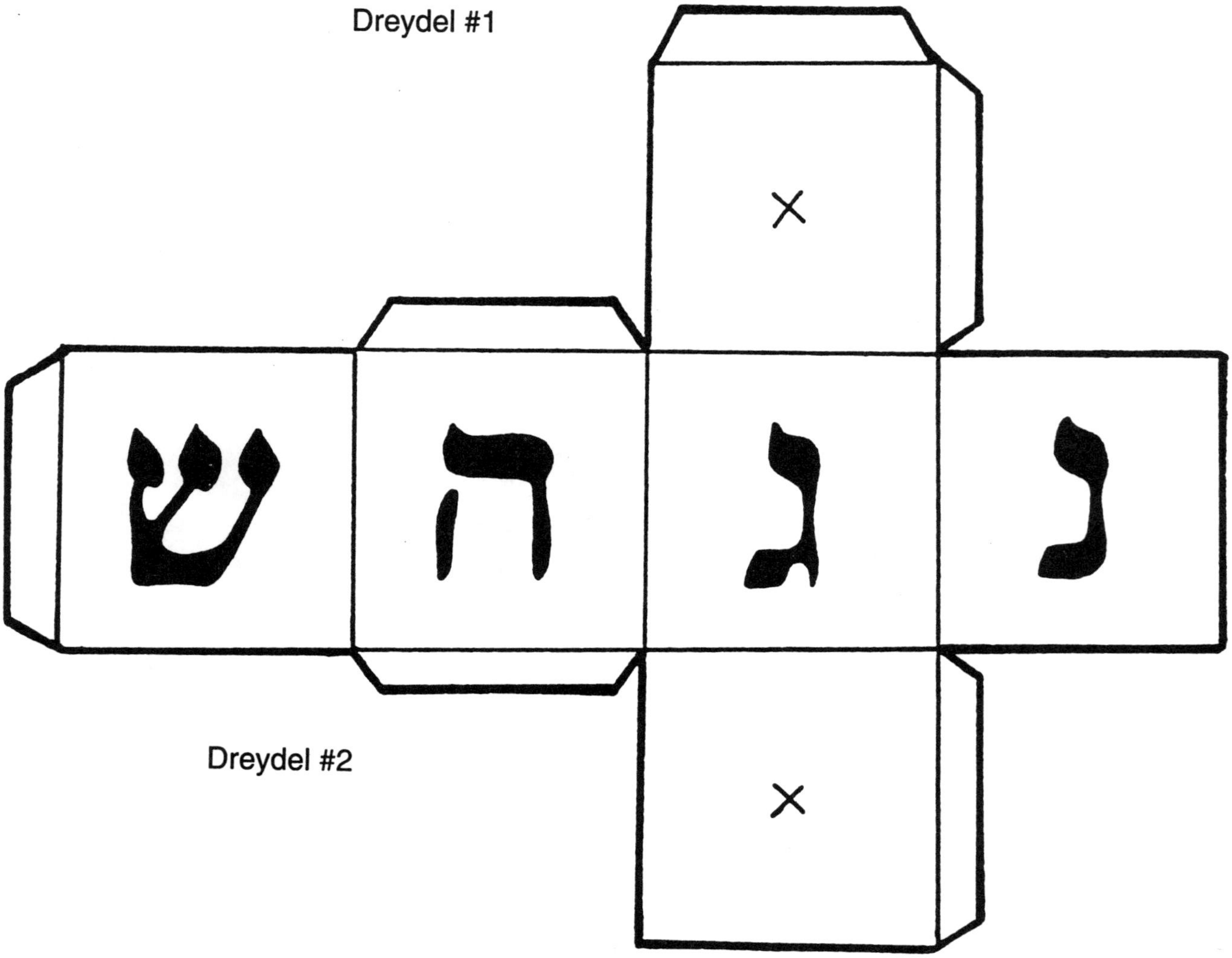

Dreydel #2

Song 15

Peanut Butter Sandwich

Use this song with these themes:

Nutrition

Cooking

Word Play

Materials to be used with these activities:

Recipe Items (see pages 62& 63)

Paper

Crayons

About This Song

Music by Raffi. Words by Raffi, Deborah Pike, Bonnie Simpson, and Bert Simpson.

Peanut Butter Sandwich is a favorite food of childhood (and of most adults if they would admit it)! Peanut butter is also a healthy food. You will find it in the protein section of the food pyramid.

Ask the children how they think peanut butter is made. The answers might surprise you. Turn the page and you can find out how to make real peanut butter with your children.

> ***A Note of Caution:*** Some children are allergic to nuts. Nut allergies can be very severe – even the touch or smell can cause a reaction. Check with the children's parents to make sure than no one in your group is allergic before using activities involving peanuts.

Peanut Butter Sandwich

Bright with Spirit

Music by Raffi
Words by Raffi, Deborah Pike, Bonnie Simpson, and Bert Simpson

How To Make Real Peanut Butter

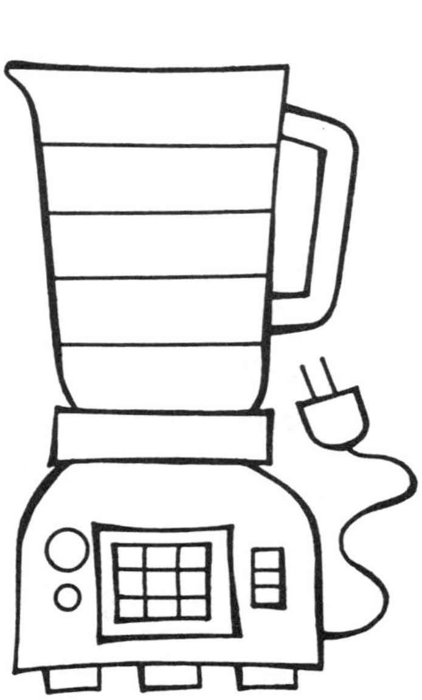

The children will love to make their own peanut butter. It is almost like magic because it is so easy to make yet it is something that most people never try. Here is how you make peanut butter:

You will need: 2 cups (474 ml) of shelled peanuts
1 to 2 tablespoons (15 to 30 ml) vegetable oil
salt
whole wheat crackers or celery sticks

What you do: Put the peanuts in a blender (small amount at a time) with the vegetable oil. Blend at medium speed until desired consistency is reached. (It may be necessary to stop and use a rubber spatula to remove the peanuts from the blender's blades once or twice.) Add salt as needed. It makes about one cup.

Let the children spread the peanut butter on crackers or celery sticks.

Peanut Butter Cookies

This is a delicious and easy recipe for making peanut butter cookies:

You will need: 1 yellow cake mix
1 cup (237 ml) peanut butter
2 eggs
1/4 cup (60 ml) water
1/4 cup (59 ml) soft margarine

What you do: Mix half of the cake mix with the other ingredients. Add the other half of the cake mix and mix with a spoon or hands. Drop by spoonfuls onto cookie sheet. Flatten cookies with a fork. Bake at 375° for 8 to 10 minutes. Makes 4 to 5 dozen cookies. This is a great recipe for feeding many people.

Make Believe Restaurant

Help the children create a "restaurant" in your learning environment, using as many props as you can find – table, chairs, paper, pencil, plates, placemats, utensils, pretend food, aprons, hats, notepads for taking orders, a cash register, play money, etc. Let the children become involved in creating the restaurant. Brainstorm ideas.

Everyone will have fun taking turns "working" in the restaurant or "dining out!"

Magic "No-Bake" Peanut Butter Cookies

This is a no-bake cookie recipe which works very well for a classroom experience (and great for home too!):

You will need:
1/2 cup (120 ml)honey
1 cup (237 ml) powdered milk
1 cup (237 ml) peanut butter
1/2 cup (119 ml) chocolate chips
1/2 cup (119 ml) coconut
1 cup (237 ml) bran flakes, crushed

What you do: Mix the first five ingredients together. Roll into balls. Roll the balls in the crushed bran flakes. Refrigerate until firm. Makes about 3 dozen cookies.

Science In A Nutshell

Children (and adults!) may be surprised to learn that peanuts are not really nuts at all. Instead of growing on trees like walnuts or pecans, they grow just under the ground – like potatoes – with leaves and yellow flowers above the surface.

Peanuts are harvested in the fall, four or five months after planting. They can be eaten raw as well as roasted. Raw peanuts (in or out of their shells) are available at many health and specialty stores. Children will enjoy comparing the look, feel, smell, and taste of raw and roasted peanuts. If you have squirrels or bluejays nearby, try offering them both kinds as well, to see if they have a preference!

Yum Yum Yummy Yum Yum

Make a classroom "wall book" of favorite foods. Begin by brainstorming – ask the children to name foods that they love to eat. Record each preference using this pattern:

__________ loves to eat __________ and __________.

Ask the children to draw their favorite foods on a paper plate or circular piece of paper. Reprint the sentences on strips of paper and mount everyone's contribution on a wall or bulletin board. Include photographs of each child if they are available.

Sherrie loves to eat crackers and soup.

Bert loves to eat apples and bananas.

A Peanut Butter and ___?___ Sandwich

On each peanut butter sandwich, draw and color "something" else you would put on your sandwich.

Song 16

Five Little Pumpkins

Use this song with these themes:

Autumn

Halloween

Plants

Ordinal Numerals

❖❖❖❖❖❖❖❖❖❖

Materials to be used with these activities:

Recipe Items (see page 66)

"Real" Pumpkin

Scooping Spoons

Jar with Lid

Votive Candle

Tagboard

Masking Tape

Yarn

Lunch-Size Paper Bags

Balloons

About This Song

Traditional

Five Little Pumpkins is a rhyme that children will love saying over and over again. On page 68, you will find patterns for the *Five Little Pumpkins.* Copy, color, and cut out. Mount them on tagboard and add a tongue depressor. They make wonderful stick puppets. The children can hide under a table and hold their puppets up to dramatize the rhyme as it is being said or sung. The patterns will also work well for a flannel or magnetic board.

Five Little Pumpkins

Pumpkin Snacks

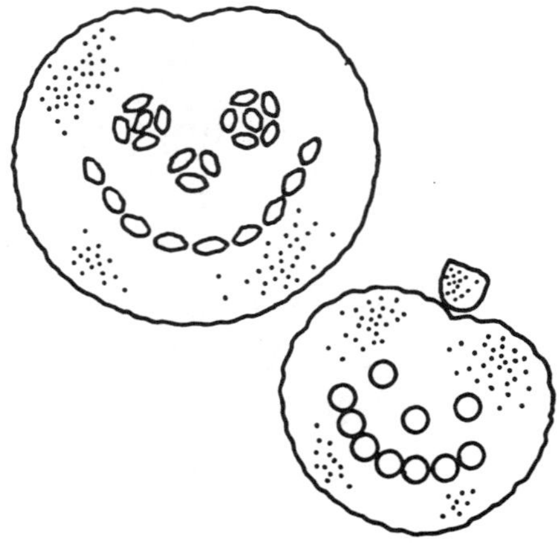

This is a fun snack idea for a Halloween party. These pumpkin snacks are very healthy and the children will be able to make them all by themselves.

What you need: Bread, spreadable cheese, butter knives, raisins.

What you do: Give each child a slice of bread. Each slice should be cut in the shape of a circle/pumpkin. The children then spread cheese all over the top surface of the bread. Raisins can be used to add facial features.

A Real Pumpkin

A real pumpkin can be used for a variety of educational experiences. Here are three ideas that you can use with one real pumpkin:

Idea 1 – **Positional Concepts**. While you are carving the pumpkin discuss the concepts of in and out. The children are taking something that is "in" the pumpkin and are taking it "out" of the pumpkin.

Idea 2 – **Science Concept**. An air supply is needed for fire to burn. Use a jar and a votive candle to demonstrate how fire needs air to burn. Leave the cover off the jar and watch the candle burn. Put on the cover back on the jar and watch the flame go out.

Idea 3 – **Cook Pumpkin Seeds**. Save the seeds from the carved pumpkin. Here is a successful recipe: 2 cups (474 ml) pumpkin seeds, 1 1/2 tablespoons (23 ml) melted butter, 1 1/2 teaspoons (7.3 ml) salt. Add the melted butter and salt to the seeds. Spread on a cookie sheet rubbed with salad oil. Bake in a 250° oven until crisp and brown, about 2 hours.

Idea 4 – **Counting Seeds.** Separate the seeds from the pulp and ask the children to guess how many seeds there are. (Suggest that the children keep their guesses "secret" so that those with little practice at estimation will not feel embarrassed by a "wild guess.") Then count the seeds singly, or try counting by two's, five's or tens!

Lacing Card

Draw a large pumpkin on a piece of tagboard. Color a face. Punch holes an inch apart, all around the edge. Using a 24 inch piece of yarn, wrap one end of the yarn with a small piece of masking tape. The masking tape will function as a safe needle. The children can "sew" their pumpkins.

Pumpkin Puppets

The children can draw and cut out pumpkins from orange construction paper. (You may want to use the patterns provided on page 68.) The eyes, nose and mouth should be cut from the pumpkin. Glue yellow construction paper across the back of the cut out spaces for the eyes, nose and mouth. Paste a small green stem at the top. Paste the finished pumpkins on lunch-size paper bags. Arms may be attached with brads.

Use the pumpkins to dramatize *Five Little Pumpkins.*

Balloon-Jack-O-Lantern Decorations

Blow up many orange balloons and tie closed. Using a black permanent magic marker, draw a Jack-o-Lantern face on each balloon. Hang the balloons from the ceiling. They make great decorations for a Halloween party.

How Does A Pumpkin Grow

Enlarge the following illustrations. Let the children use these cards to sequence the growth of a pumpkin. You can make a double set of these cards and the children can use them to play concentration.

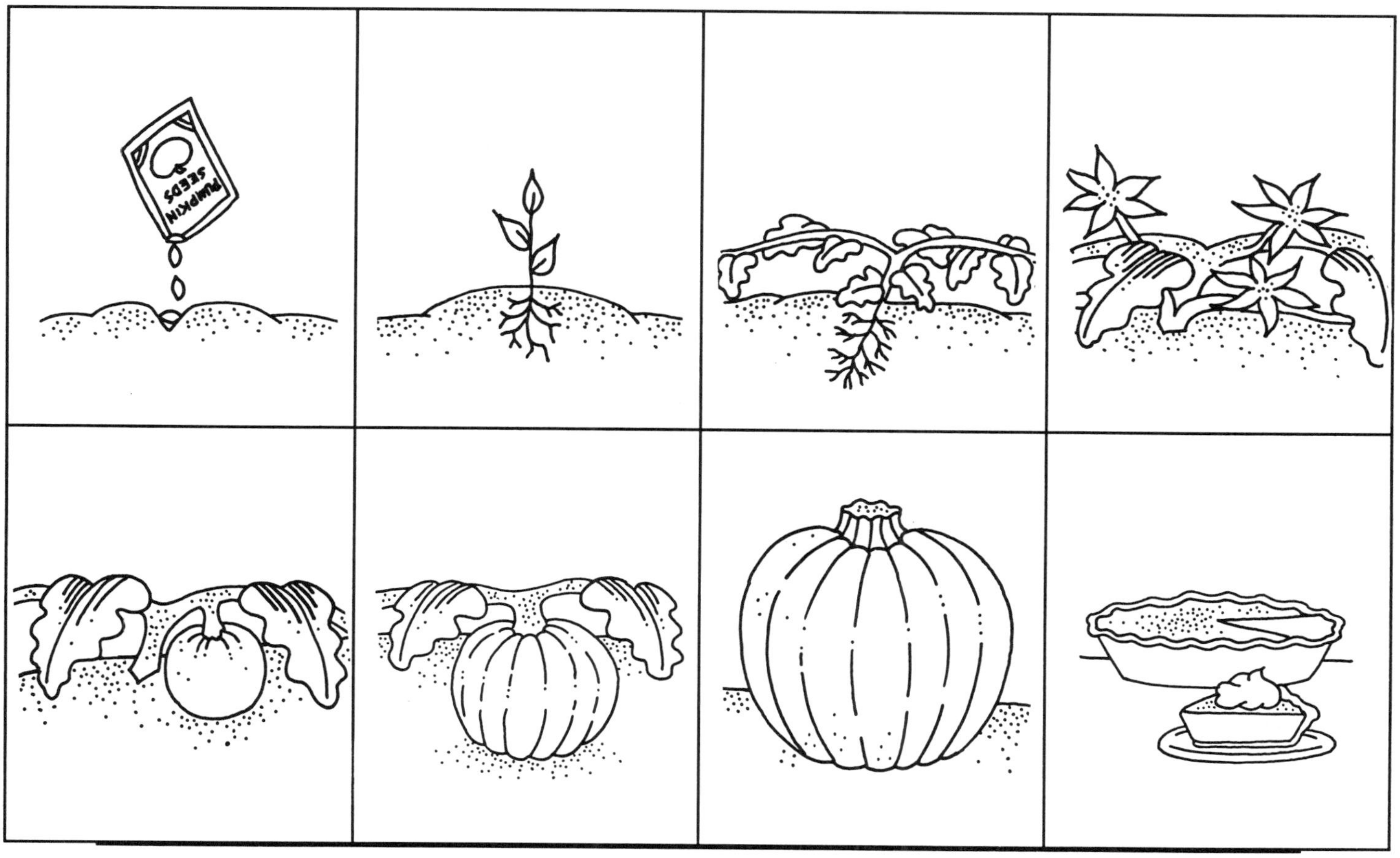

Follow the instructions found on page 65.

Song 17

The Sharing Song

Use this song with these themes:

Sharing

Body Parts

Self-Esteem

Friendship

Materials to be used with these activities:

Photocopies of Children's Photographs

Contact Paper or Laminate

Paper

Scissors

Crayons

Art Scraps

Jigsaw Puzzle

Paint

Cardboard

Toilet Paper Tubes

Glitter/Ribbons

Spray Shellac

Sequins

About This Song

Music by Raffi. Words by Raffi, D. Pike, and Bonnie Simpson & Bert Simpson

Early childhood and sharing are two concepts that do not always go well together. Learning to share is probably one of a young child's greatest accomplishments.

Many children think about sharing. Here are some of their thoughts: "It's so much fun to have things that are 'mine!' Why should I give my things away? Will I have to give it up forever? Will I ever see my things again?"

In *The Sharing Song*, Raffi sings "It's mine but you can have some. With you I'd like to share it, "cause if I share it with you, you'll have some too!" This song shows children the joy one can receive in sharing. An important lifetime lesson!

The Sharing Song

With a lilt

Music by Raffi

Words by Raffi, Deborah Pike, Bonnie Simpson, and Bert Simpson

Learning to share is a difficult task in the early years. The following activities are designed to help children learn the joys of sharing and giving.

A Puzzle of Me

This is a delightful activity that can be made as a gift for a grandparent or for a special friend. It's a wonderful gift that may be hard to part with!

The "puzzle of me" is easy-to-make. Have each child find a favorite photograph of themselves. Enlarge the photo on a copy machine (200% if possible). On the back of the photo write a special message to the person who will be receiving the puzzle. (Have younger children dictate the message.) Laminate or cover in clear contact paper both sides of the photocopied picture.

Cut the picture into six or eight pieces. Put the pieces in an envelope and send to the person of the child's choice.

What is Sharing?

Many children think sharing is simply giving up something. Sharing is also a problem-solving skill. Ask the children to choose a partner. The partners will be making an art project together. Give each pair one piece of paper, one pair of scissors, one bottle of glue, one box of crayons, and multiple scraps of colored construction paper.

Tell the children that they are each to make an art project. If they plan carefully and work together there will be enough materials. They will have to share the materials. Demonstrate how to share by cutting a piece of paper in two.

Let the children finish creating their projects by sharing the materials you gave them.

Puzzle Picture Frames

This is a wonderful gift to make. You will need two 7" x 9" (178 mm x 229 mm) rectangles of corrugated cardboard. Cut a 5" x 7" (127mm x 178 mm) opening in the center of one of the pieces of cardboard. Using a discarded jigsaw puzzle, let the children, with supervision ***(and following the safety directions on the cans)*** spray the puzzle pieces with an acrylic paint and then spray on a shellac.

Using the painted puzzle pieces, have the children cover the cardboard rectangle. Instruct the children to overlap and mix the different colored pieces around the frame's edge. When the child is pleased with the arrangement, the pieces can be glued in place. Glue the two cardboard pieces together (front and back of the frame along three sides only.) Leave one side gluefree so they can slide a picture into the frame.

Sharing Ideas

A tremendous way for children to learn is by sharing ideas. We can accomplish more and develop better ideas when we ask many people to share what they think. Writing poetry is a good way to show children a concrete example of sharing ideas.

Ask the children to help you write an acrostic poem. Even very young children will be able to participate in this activity. Write the word SHARING down the side of chart paper or on a a blackboard. Have the children think of a word or sentence that begins with each of the letters in the word "sharing" that could represent something about the concept of sharing. For example, the "S" could be "Sometimes Tim and I play with my toys together." "H" "Happily, I give you my ball."

Microphone Magic

A pretend microphone can become an effective tool for building confidence and self-esteem. Here is a fun art activity where all the children can make their own microphones. Each child will need a toilet paper tube. Decorate with paint, glitter, and ribbons. The fancier the microphone, the more extroverted the young performer might become.

When the microphone is finished is when the fun really begins. Play *The Sharing Song* and let the children share the center stage! One at a time, have a child pretend that she/he is Raffi singing *The Sharing Song* (naturally the child will sing holding her/his microphone).

On the recording when the children's voices join Raffi's, the other children in the group may join in. Wow! Sharing the stage as Raffi is pretty exciting!

Sharing the Spot Light - King or Queen for a Day!

Let the children create their own crown. Crown pattern can be found on page 72. Decorate the crown with anything and everything that you keep in your art box – buttons, sequins, glitter, gems, markers, paint, ribbon, ricrac, etc. When the crowns are finished, ask the children to think of a friend that they would like to crown as king or queen for the day. The children will share their crown for a day by letting another child wear it. At the end of the day the children may bring their own crowns home.

The Crown Pattern

Activity suggestions for the crown pattern are found on page 71.

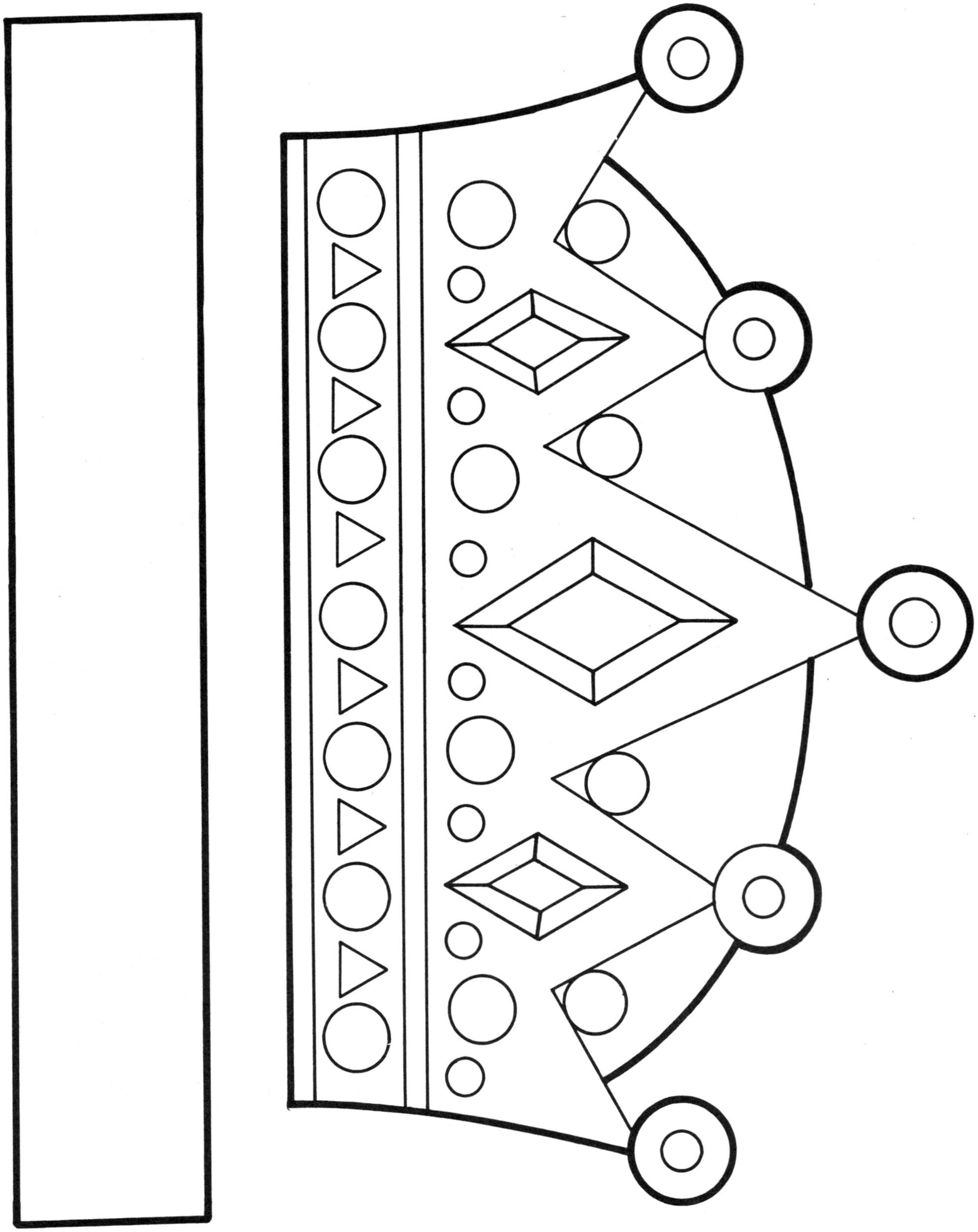

Song 18

Mr. Sun

Use this song with these themes:

Summer

Weather

Positional Concepts

❖❖❖❖❖❖❖❖❖❖

Materials to be used with these activities:

Construction Paper

Small Classroom Objects

Bubble Recipe (see page 74)

Tissue Paper

Paint

Cardboard

Crayons

Glue

Brad

Craft Sticks

Fresh Fruit

White paint

Straws

About This Song

Traditional

Mr. Sun is a cheerful song with easy-to-learn lyrics and an upbeat melody. It is one of those special songs – the kind of song that makes one hum the melody all day long! This song reminds us of the fun of playing outside on a beautiful sunny day – just one of the small joys of childhood. So. *Mr. Sun,* please shine down on me!

Mr. Sun

Sun Bleached Paper

Talk about the sun with the children. Why do we need the sun? Brainstorm all the important ways that the sun is important to us.

Next, have the children perform an experiment/art project. (This project is like magic to a small child.) Write each child's name on a piece of colored construction paper. Set the paper outside in the sun. Have the children place a number of objects onto their piece of paper. Leave the paper outside all day. The children will be excited to find the picture that results when the sun bleaches the paper around the objects, but not the areas under the objects.

Bubbles

Bubbles are an essential for early childhood. The wonder and fun at blowing bubbles, chasing bubbles and popping bubbles is indescribable. Here is a successful recipe for making your own bubbles:

- 1/4 cup (60 ml) glycerin (found at the pharmacy)
- 1/2 cup (120 ml) water
- 1 tablespoon (15 ml) liquid detergent

Mix all the ingredients in a jar and let the child use a bubble pipe or straw to blow bubbles.

This is a great outside project for a warm, sunny day!

Learn About The Real Sun

Provide each of the children with red, orange, yellow, and white tissue paper, cut into 2" (51 mm) squares; scissors; glue; bowls; water; paintbrushes; and, pencils.

Let the children describe the sun. Give each child a large piece of yellow construction paper and have them cut a large circle from the paper. Set out bowls of watered-down glue, paint brushes, and the tissue paper squares.

Using the paintbrush, the children should cover the entire yellow paper circle with the watered-down glue. Let the children place the tissue paper on the circle. After the children have filled the entire yellow circle with the tissue paper, the children can carefully paint over the tissue paper with the glue mixture. This will give the entire sun a "shiny" look.

Weather Wheel

Children love to make weather wheels. Each of the children may each make their own weather wheel from "Chinet" paper plates, or you can make a large poster board weather wheel to be used in the classroom or home school environment.

The weather wheel should be divided into five sections. In each of the five sections draw or glue a picture of a sunny day, rainy day, cloudy day, snowy day, and a windy day. Cut out an arrow from a plastic margarine or coffee can lid. Attach the arrow to the center of the wheel using a brad. The children describe the weather of the day and move the arrow to point to their choice.

No Fuss Frozen Fruit Pops

On hot sunny days children like to eat a lot of cold frozen treats. Here is a healthy snack that will cool even the "hottest" child, while also providing them with something "good" to eat.

You will need: craft sticks, fresh fruit, pineapple rings, whole strawberries, bananas, and watermelon. Have the children slide the craft stick into the pieces of fruit. Cover the fruit with plastic wrap and place in the freezer for at least two hours. What a great treat! (And no mess!)

Cloud Pictures

The most beautiful clouds are those that we see on a sunny day – the big, white, fluffy cirrus clouds. Let the children lie on the grass and look up at the clouds as they float overhead. Look at all the different shapes. Do they see anything that resembles something familiar in those shapes – possibly a dog, a dinosaur, or a mountain?

Once you give young children one or two ideas it is amazing all the things that they think they see. It is also fun to lay in the grass and sing *Mr. Sun.* He certainly will be shining down upon you.

Bring the children indoors and give them a piece of light blue construction paper, straws, and thin white paint. Have them spoon some paint onto the center of the paper. Using the straw, blow the paint across the paper. Encourage the children to blow the paint in all different directions. The idea is for the children to try and create some of the clouds that they saw outdoors. Label the picture with the name of the object the child thinks the "cloud" resembles.

Mr Sun Pattern

Let each child create their own Mr. Sun. This can be used as a prop when the children sing *Mr. Sun.* Hide the sun behind your back when you get to the line "hiding behind a tree." Hold the sun over your head when you sing the line "Please shine down on me."

Song 19

Old MacDonald Had A Band

Use this song with these themes:

Musical Instruments

Memory Skills

Sequencing

❖❖❖❖❖❖❖❖❖❖

Materials to be used with these activities:

Paper Towel Tubes

Waxpaper

Hanger

Bottle Caps

Wood Blocks

Craft Sticks

String/Bells

Pie Tins

Ribbon/Glue

Shoe Box

Wrapping Paper Tube

About This Song

Traditional, adapted by Raffi and Ken Whiteley

Old MacDonald Had A Farm is a song that is taught to all children during the early childhood years. After spending so much time singing the traditional version of this song, the children will delight in learning another way to sing a favorite song. Listen to Raffi's version of *Old MacDonald Had A Band.* The children will instantly be able to sing the lyrics.

> The following pages will give you a multitude of ideas for making your own musical instruments. Have the children choose what instruments they would like to make. Let the children name the instrument. When everyone is ready, they can sing *Old MacDonald Had A Band* and use their own instruments.

Old MacDonald Had A Band

Traditional
Adapted and arranged
Raffi & Ken Whiteley

Special Safety Notice: Although these musical instrument are fun to play with, many of them contain small parts. If you are using these instruments with children under the age of four, please supervise! It is often too tempting to put something in a mouth that shouldn't be there!

Shakers

You will need paper towel cardboard tubes. Let the children decorate the tubes. Place bean seeds, rice, buttons, or anything else that you have on hand that would create a shaking sound inside the tube. Seal the ends of the tubes with several layers of wax paper and rubber bands.

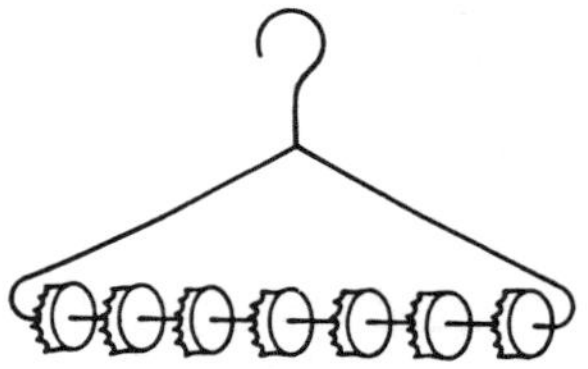

Clanging Bottle Caps

Bottle caps strung on a coat hanger make an interesting sound. An adult will have to pound a hole in the center of the bottle caps with a hammer and nail. Children can string the caps onto the hanger.

Clatter Cups

Using paper or plastic cups, decorate the outside of the cups. Place marbles, beans, etc. inside the cups and duct tape the two together.

Wood Block

Using a piece of wood, saw ridges across it. This wood block may be played by scraping a popsicle stick across the ridges. You can also pound in two nails and string a rubber band. Strum the rubber band and for a guitar sound.

Paper Plate Tambourine

Punch holes near the edge of two paper plates. (For best results use sturdy paper plates.) Tie the two plates together with string and bells. When you play this instrument you will hear two sounds.

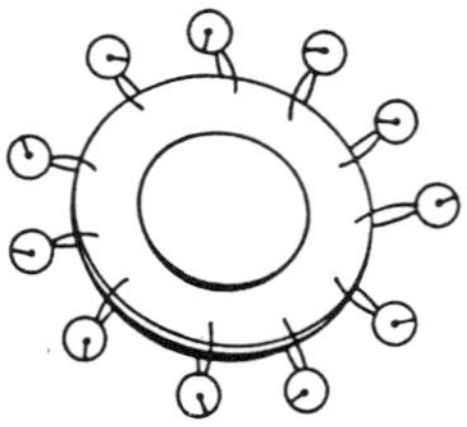

Pie Tin Tambourine

Here is another version of an easy-to-make tambourine that makes a sound different from the paper plate tambourine. Punch five holes near the edge with a paper punch. Add ribbon, string for decoration, and jingle bells for sound.

Shoe Box Guitar

Cut out a hole in the center of the lid of a shoe box. Place the lid back on the box. Stretch rubber bands across the box as shown.

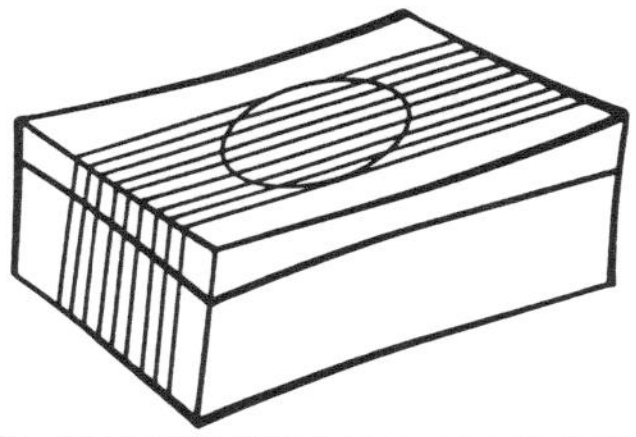

Drums

Version 1: No band is complete without drums. Large coffee cans with both ends cut out and plastic lids attached to each end work very well.

Version 2: Another creative idea for a drum is using a 1 pound coffee can filled 1/3 with water. Stretch an inner tube over the top and tied on tightly with heavy rubber binders.

Rain Sticks

Every child will need a wrapping paper tube. Decorate the tube with paint, tissue paper, crayons, etc. Cover one end of the tube with wax paper and a rubber band. Fill with rice. Cover the other end with wax paper and a rubber band.

The children will love holding the rain stick and experimenting with the sounds of the rice running from one end of the tube to the other.

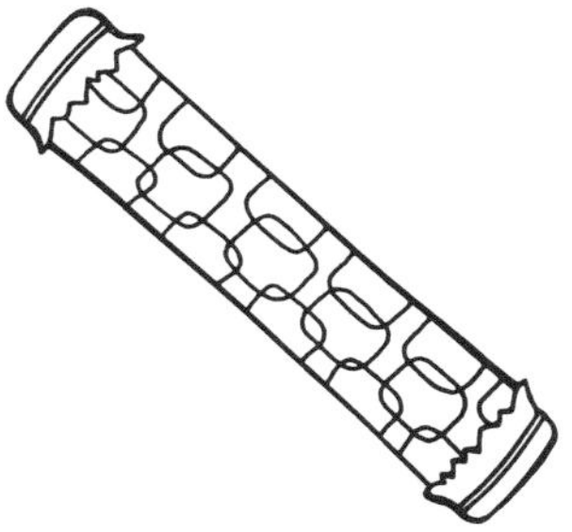

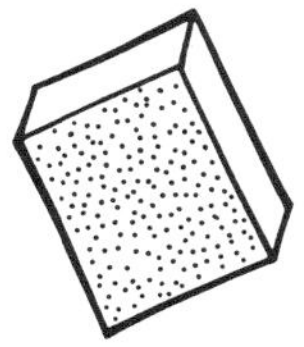

Sandpaper Blocks

This instrument is made by gluing sandpaper to two small blocks. A scratching rhythm can be created when the two blocks are rubbed together.

Maracas

Version 1: Carefully cut the portion of the egg carton that holds the eggs. Put some stones, unpopped popcorn or other dry hard objects that will make noise into the cartons. Poke a hole in the bottom of one of the cartons and put a tongue depressor or pencil in the hole for a handle. Tape the two pieces of the carton together.

Using newspaper strips, dip them into wheat paste or liquid starch and cover the cartons making sure that the handle is anchored into the cartons. After the maraca is dry, it may be painted.

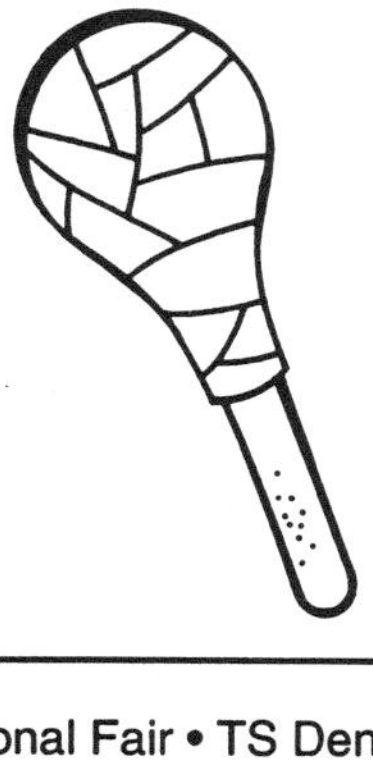

Version 2: Use a discarded lightbulb. Tape a tongue depressor to the metal stem of the light bulb. Cover the light bulb and the taped section of the tongue depressor with paper mache. Allow to dry. Gently tape the maraca on the edge of a desk. The light bulb will break inside the paper mache, leaving the glass to make the sounds inside the maraca. Paint.

Old MacDonald Had A Band

Enlarge the patterns, color, cut out, and back with self-stick velcro to use on the flannel board. The visual presentation will help the children maintain the proper sequence of the musical instruments in the song.